The Poetry of Grace

The Poetry of Grace

Reformation Themes and Structures in
English Seventeenth-Century Poetry

by William H. Halewood

New Haven and London, Yale University Press

Originally published with assistance from
the foundation established in memory of Amaza Stone Mather
of the Class of 1907, Yale College.
Copyright © 1970 by Yale University.
Second printing, 1972.
Library of Congress catalog card number: 75–115370
International Standard Book Number: 0–300–0134–8

Designed by Marvin Howard Simmons,
set in Baskerville type,
and printed in the United States of America by
The Carl Purington Rollins Printing-Office
of the Yale University Press, New Haven, Connecticut.

Published in Great Britain, Europe, and Africa by
Yale University Press, Ltd., London.
Distributed in Canada by McGill-Queen's University Press, Montreal;
in Latin America by Kaiman & Polon, Inc., New York City;
in India by UBS Publishers' Distributors Pvt., Ltd., Delhi;
in Japan by John Weatherhill, Inc., Tokyo.

To Deane

The condition of Man after the fall of *Adam* is such, that he cannot turn and prepare himself, by his own natural strength and good works, to faith, and calling upon God. Wherefore we have no power to do good works pleasant and acceptable to God, without the Grace of God by Christ preventing us, that we may have a good will, and working with us when we have that good will.

Article X, *The Thirty-Nine Articles of the Church of England*

Beyond compare the Son of God was seen
Most glorious, in him all his Father shone
Substantially express'd, and in his face
Divine compassion visibly appear'd,
Love without end, and without measure grace

Paradise Lost, III, 138–42

Contents

Preface

Some readers will find a certain dull mischief in the plan
of this book, which seems to aim rather at a blurring than
a clarification of distinctions, purposing to undermine
the exclusivity of such standard classifications as *metaphysical, Miltonic, Puritan,* and *Arminian* and making
a general chorus of poets who deserve to be heard sep-
arately. One feels little regret at having, perhaps, played
fast and loose with standard classifications, which must
stand or fall according to their serviceability—and which
will not be made to fall in any case by a single effort to
revise them. The possibility that the poets may have been
made all to sing one note seems a more serious matter.
I hope this has not happened. It is not a necessary consequence of using poems to illustrate theses, as Louis
Martz and Rosamond Tuve have sensitively and scrupu-
lously shown—often with the same poems I have used—
and there is, of course, the insistent individuality of the
poems themselves in constant operation against it. Still,
an essay proposing to treat a problem of "period style"
necessarily commits itself to generalization, and to the
hope that attention to species will not be taken for indifference to individuals.

My debts to other students of the period are numerous and only sketchily recorded—which is especially the case in the chapter on *Paradise Lost,* where it seemed necessary to travel light just to get through. Several omissions now seem regrettable, including a failure to proclaim my admiration for Stanley E. Fish's *Surprised by Sin: The Reader in Paradise Lost,* a book which did not appear in time to guide my own attempt to read Milton by Reformation light, but with which I deeply agree. I am pleased to corroborate some of its major findings.

I was greatly helped in beginning this work by a generous fellowship grant from the American Council of Learned Societies, for which I am very grateful. Colleagues and students have also helped generously. My friend Marvin Levich of the philosophy department of Reed College is a critic of arguments who has made various improvements in the order of this one. Daniel Deegan, another friend in the same department, assisted with theological expertise and with loans from his theological library. University of Toronto graduate students enrolled in a "Poetry of Grace" seminar have helped refine the materials and propositions of which the book is made; undergraduates in my seventeenth-century survey classes have tolerantly consented to learn a great deal more about Reformation theology than they wanted to. I am indebted to Professor Louis L. Martz, who read the manuscript for the Yale University Press, for suggestions which have made the final product both more civil and more shapely.

The dedication expresses my gratitude to my wife for grace under pressure.

W. H. H.

University College
University of Toronto
March 1970

Introduction: A Modern Problem

As several studies have shown, the modern vogue for
Donne and the metaphysicals began in an enthusiastic
confusion which assimilated them to twentieth-century
movements of realism and naturalism.[1] Donne, especially, seemed to lend himself readily to such "kidnapping," as it was called in one scholarly protest, by his
forthright treatment of sex, his resolutely colloquial dic-
tion, his seeming fidelity to the actual processes of the
mind.[2] Thus to Edmund Gosse, for example, Donne's
affinities seemed clear:

> A rigid adherence to topics and objects familiar to
> the non-poetical reader of the moment is strictly ob-
> served . . . he was in a totally new and unprecedented
> sense, a realist. In this he revolted with success against
> all the procedure of the Renaissance, and is, in his

1. The only complete study of the metaphysical revival is Joseph
E. Duncan, *The Revival of Metaphysical Poetry* (Minneapolis, 1959).
2. Merritt Hughes, "Kidnapping Donne," *California Essays in
Criticism*, 2d ser., 4 (Berkeley, 1934): 61–92.

turbid and unskilful way, the forerunner of modern naturalism in English poetry.[3]

That Donne should be regarded as turbid and unskilful now seems a curious mistake, but the general insistence that he was a proto-modern having intimate connections with modern realism resulted in other distortions no less improbable. An American critic saw him as "a Whitman born in Shakespeare's time,"[4] and the view that Donne's weltanschauung was that of modern radical skepticism at one time flourished vigorously and has made intermittent appearances throughout the period of the metaphysical revival.

Such errors, when openly committed, have been learnedly and energetically overthrown. There is evidence, however, of their continued vitality in certain fundamental assumptions of the poetic theory which gives the modern critic his standard means of approach to the metaphysicals and to most contemporary poetry, and which in turn appears to derive leading principles from a special kind of reading of the metaphysicals as "realists." It is rash to generalize about modern poetic theory, and the part of it which is of primary concern in this study—its conception of form—is that about which generalization is perhaps most difficult. René Wellek exaggerates little in saying that "it would be easy to collect hundreds of definitions of 'form' and 'structure' from contemporary critics and aestheticians and to show that they contradict each other so radically and basically that it may be best to abandon the terms."[5] Yet it seems clear, in the midst of this confusion, that there is almost general assent to certain propositions treating form and structure

3. *The Life and Letters of John Donne*, 2 vols. (London, 1899), 2:340.

4. See Duncan, *Metaphysical Poetry*, p. 126.

5. *Concepts of Criticism* (New Haven, 1963), pp. 54–68.

on a theoretical level and that these propositions operate as unquestioned assumptions in a great deal of the workaday activity of critics and scholars, particularly in their dealings with metaphysical poetry. I have in mind the doctrine of "opposites" for which critics regularly cite the now famous passage in Coleridge's *Biographia Literaria* describing the operation of the unifying imagination:

> Imagination . . . reveals itself in the balance or reconciliation of opposite or discordant qualities: of sameness, with differences; of the general with the concrete; the idea, with the image; the individual, with the representative; the sense of novelty and of freshness, with old and familiar objects; a more than usual state of emotion, with more than usual order; judgement ever awake and steady self-possession, with enthusiasm and feeling profound or vehement.

It has become a commonplace relentlessly repeated in the discussion and exegesis of metaphysical poetry as well as in modern critical theory that a poem is a structure of opposites, a system of contrary meanings held in tension, and Coleridge serves standardly as authority for that position. In the context of Coleridge's critical thought, however, the passage falls into place as an example of his characteristic insistence on the combining power of the imaginative faculty, on the "aspect of union" constantly stressed in his "organistic" theory. What has been notable in the appearances of the passage in twentieth-century criticism from the first—and its first appearances coincided with the beginnings of the modern revival of the metaphysicals—has been its isolation from this context and conversion to the uses of a theory which has determinedly cut itself off from philosophical monisms of any kind and devoted itself to aspects of disunion. T. S. Eliot's 1921 essay on Marvell, which launched the passage

on its modern career and gave hints of its susceptibility
to modern distortion, also showed how it might be used
in defining the qualities of a metaphysical poet.[6] The
marriage of "opposites theory" and metaphysical poetry
was thus prepared, with results that constitute a major
datum of the literary history of our time.

The anachronism in this process as it applies to Coleridge has been detected.[7] The anachronism in the treatment of the metaphysicals, I believe, has not, though it
would seem plain that modern opposites theory is a
version of realist theory, and hence as dubious a bridge
to seventeenth-century poets as Gosse's crude connection
via the "topics and objects" of realism. But the parallel,
or coincidence, of opposites theory in poetics and procedures legislated in some of the major formulations of
the theory of realistic fiction has an interest of its own,
and it will be useful to suggest some analogues in the
theory of the novel to Eliot's seminal statement for
poetics in his essay on Marvell. There, in some well-
known sentences which almost convert Coleridge's argument for the imagination of unity into an argument for
the imagination of disunity, he described a poetical con-
sciousness which could include "a recognition in the expression of every experience of other kinds of experience
which are possible." Surely, we are very near in this to the
claim familiar in the manifestos of realism that honest
dealing in novels requires the novelist to accept the full
complexity of experience and not to simplify or manip-
ulate its contradictions.[8]

6. *Selected Essays, 1917–1932* (New York, 1932), pp. 251–63.

7. See William K. Wimsatt, Jr., and Cleanth Brooks, *Literary
Criticism: A Short History* (New York, 1957), pp. 395–401.

8. It was, above all, the concerns of the novel which dominated
critical discussion in the first decades of this century, and to such

Ford Madox Ford, for example, provides one of the major texts for the position in his insistence that "the novelist must not, by taking sides, exhibit his preferences. . . . He has . . . to render, and not to tell." The position at its simplest calls for mere noninterference. It appears fairly simply in Henry James: "In proportion as in what [fiction] offers us we see life without rearrangement do we feel that we are touching the truth; in proportion as we see it with rearrangement do we feel that we are being put off with a substitute, a compromise, a convention." Nonsimplification is the basis of "truth" in the realistic novel, and Eliot takes the same ground for poetry when he (somewhat implausibly) condemns in "The Use of Poetry" the simplifying "doctrine" of Shelley's poetry while accepting Dante's doctrine as "founded on the facts of experience." Cleanth Brooks makes the application to metaphysical poetry, which he distinguishes as a poetry in which "the poet has been just to the complexity

---

an extent as to make plausible the suggestion that even Coleridge's definition of the imagination would be read in their light. The "opposites" had, of course, an extensive pre-novel and pre-Coleridge history. Aristotle's conception of tragedy as a mode combining pity and terror, bringing together, as I. A. Richards has put it, "the impulse to approach and the impulse to withdraw," is clearly a version of opposites theory. Another is Dr. Johnson's definition of metaphysical wit as a *discordia concors;* "The most heterogeneous ideas . . . yoked by violence together." Another version appears in the giant paradoxes of Blake's ethic and poetic of "contraries." To these named landmarks of critical theory should be added the aesthetic formulas calling for variety in unity and unity in variety that can be found in every period and on both sides of a good many critical arguments (reflected, for example, in a typical period disguise, in the Augustan debate over the rival claims of genius and the rules). As a specific stimulus to Eliot's conception of opposites, it should be recalled that he himself considered that he was appreciating the poetry of the metaphysicals in terms appropriate to French symbolism.

of experience and has not given us an abstraction in the
guise of experience."[9]

But we are clearly getting into considerations which go
beyond artistic process in poems and novels, and which
open the way again to the matter of "topics and objects."
For the "truth" of the realistic novel is of a different order
from the "truth" of metaphysical poetry and would seem
to be of a kind that can better stand being left in complexity, unrearranged and unabstracted, and is perhaps
only convincing as truth when thus handled. The truth
of the metaphysicals, on the contrary, must appear, especially to the modern secular intelligence, as accessible
only to the processes of abstraction and rearrangement.
The difference between them may be simply described
and involves no novelties of theory or interpretation.
Typically, modern realism has accepted the limits of a
"social vision," and the complexities which it has represented have been those of human relationships and
human institutions; its "problems," large and small, have
been basically ethical, and its roots can more reasonably
be sought in the eighteenth century than in the seventeenth. The vision of the metaphysicals, on the other
hand, while obviously not excluding the area of human
relationships, consistently suggests a larger background
for them than the merely ethical. Human destiny and
divine providence, grace, salvation, mortality, and sin
form the context in which the human event occurs, and
the event is modified by its context ("And into ashes all
our lust"). In the religious poetry of the metaphysicals
this background becomes foreground, and context be-

9. Ford, *The English Novel from the Earliest Days to the Death
of Joseph Conrad* (London, 1930), pp. 128–29; James, "The Art of
Fiction," *Henry James: Selected Fiction*, ed. Leon Edel (New York,
1953), p. 601; Eliot, *Use of Poetry* (Cambridge, Mass., 1933), p. 96;
Brooks, *Modern Poetry and the Tradition* (London, 1948), p. 53.

comes subject. The truth involved is a truth not of social but of spiritual experience, or, in another sense, not of experience at all but of faith—which, far from contenting itself with the raw data of existence, determinedly simplifies and abstracts to expose a geometry of ultimate meanings. One does not mean to imply, of course, that realistic novelists are necessarily indifferent to ultimate meanings (a notion which the example of such writers as Graham Greene and Albert Camus suffices easily to overturn); however, the involvement of realistic fiction with people in society, with the social surface of life, has been so extended and thoroughgoing as to make the conception of the religious novel, as a genre, appear almost a contradiction in terms.

It will have become clear by now that in the bias of the present study the term "metaphysical" has a more than conventional application to the poetry conventionally designated by it. Objection can, of course, be made to a description of the metaphysicals as poets whose concerns are metaphysical in a literal—or philosophical—sense on the ground that other poets, not usually described with the term—the Romantics, for example—have similar concerns. Such an objection has been urged against Sir Herbert Grierson's definition of metaphysical poetry as a kind of poetry "inspired by a philosophical conception of the universe and the role assigned to the human spirit in the great drama of existence."[10] A critic has asked

10. *Metaphysical Lyrics and Poems of the Seventeenth Century* (Oxford, 1921), p. xiii. More extended attempts to discuss this poetry as "metaphysical" in the philosophical sense of the word include James Smith's essay "On Metaphysical Poetry," in *Determinations*, ed. F. R. Leavis (London, 1934), pp. 10–45 (see below, chap. 1, n. 1); S. L. Bethell, "The Nature of Metaphysical Wit," *Northern Miscellany of Literary Criticism*, 1 (1953): 19–40, reprinted in *Discussions of Donne*, ed. Frank Kermode (Boston, 1962); J. A. Mazzeo, "A Seventeenth-Century Theory of Metaphysical Poetry"

whether this cannot equally be said of Shelley's *Prome-
theus Unbound*.[11] It can, to be sure; yet the example
suggests a difference, for Shelley's "philosophical conception of the universe and the role assigned to the human
spirit" is not theological and concedes nothing to faith.
It is framed in terms of a skeptical, eclectic mythology
which challenges the nature of things from a point of
view philosophically solipsistic and hostile to orthodox
religious explanations. Shelley, and the Romantic poets
typically, while craving a vision which would make them
less forlorn, decline to be consoled by the system of beliefs
which consoles Donne and makes its presence felt everywhere in the poetry of the seventeenth century. It is
evident that the "spirit of the time" offered different sets
of possibilities to poets in 1620 and 1820.

The possibilities of which modern realism has been
aware are, of course, closer to Shelley's than to Donne's,
and they are responsible for some major confusions about
the informing intentions of seventeenth-century poetry.
The point may be illustrated by considering the problem
of resolution or reconciliation, the process by which the
tensional poem deals with its tensions and by which the
opposition of opposites is prevented from resulting in
incoherence. Critics use the terms resolution and reconciliation loosely, but generally mean by them a kind of
nonsimplifying structural balancing of alternatives consistent with the modern realist's view of the contradictory
nature of existence. That a poet of the seventeenth century might view his poetic necessities somewhat differ-

---

and "Metaphysical Poetry and the Poetic of Correspondence," in
Renaissance and Seventeenth-Century Studies (New York, 1964),
pp. 29–59.
    11. Leonard Unger, *Donne's Poetry and Modern Criticism*
(Chicago, 1950), p. 4.

ently would seem not to need arguing, but the question can be illuminated with the aid of a set of distinctions made by the English philosopher Ronald W. Hepburn. Hepburn's essay, "Poetry and Religious Belief,"[12] distinguishes four different reconciling strategies—or situations —which may occur in poetry and their analogues in human experience:

(a) Reconciliation brought about by correction, or access of new information:

> One's attitude towards a friend or lover may be ambivalent. Affection and confidence perhaps are in conflict with mistrust and jealousy. Such a conflict can usually be settled by decisive information concerning the person's behavior. Cases in which jealousy and suspicion remain after the completest possible vindication are normally classed as pathological. ... Attitudes are altered in response to knowledge of fact.

(b) Reconciliation by seeing steadily:

> With very intractable material a conflict may not be solved but only made manageable, controllable by seeing it honestly as it is, maybe by the provision of a poetic image which in its small compass holds together the warring elements. The symbol does not release the tension, but yet gives some kind of "command" over the conflict. It makes resignation possible to a greater degree than before, produces a "distancing" of the conflict that brings a measure of detachment. Such a symbol is that at the end of Yeats' "The Second Coming," the monster slouching

12. In Stephen Toulmin, Ronald W. Hepburn, and Alasdair MacIntyre, *Metaphysical Beliefs: Three Essays* (London, 1957), pp. 144–46.

toward Bethlehem to be born, in which are juxta-
posed widely conflicting ideas—the horror of the im-
minent new birth, and the innocent and holy association of the old.

(c) Reconciliation by value assertion:

If a tragedy enables us to see moral dignity in the
face of death's wastefulness, the level at which reconciliation is affected is the level of value-assertion.

(d) Reconciliation by appeal to an extrapoetic model
or reconciliation. Certain kinds of religious symbolism,
for example, have their own integrating energy, make
their own assertion of reconciliation:

The reconciliation at the close of Eliot's *Four
Quartets* faithfully expresses a reconciliation which
takes place (or shall take place) in the world. Eliot
is not rendering bearable the unresolvable conflicts
of our experience by furnishing an image which
holds them at arm's length and helps us to cope
with them with greater detachment and resignation:
he is claiming that the conflicts shall be resolved, and
his image is an image of their resolution.

Hepburn's distinctions are not wire-drawn, but they
go a good deal beyond what most literary critics would
attempt. His greater completeness, however, is in part a
consequence of his willingness to accept for poetry some
kinds of reconciliation that, by and large, modern criticism has not wanted to accept. The reconciliations allowed
for by the promoters of the poetics of opposites, from
I. A. Richards to Murray Krieger, belong to Hepburn's
second class, in which control of conflict is achieved
"by seeing it honestly as it is, maybe by the provision of
a poetic image which in its small compass holds together

the warring elements." They are such reconciliations as consist with realism's view of the world, reconciliations in which tension is maintained, not done away with, as by the triumph of one alternative or collapse of the other. And such reconciliations are required to be achieved *in* the poem, by the logical, or plausible, development of its ideas, symbols and images: "new information" as in Hepburn's (a) or outside help as in (d) are both, in this perspective, unwelcome varieties of the deus ex machina.

Hepburn's toleration of these kinds of reconciliation follows from his conception of poetry as a partner of religion in the purpose "to integrate, to make whole, men's lives, to redeem them from bewildering meaninglessness, from the futility of a life seen as a patternless succession of one happening after another." Religious poetry in his view is a special case of reconciliation or integration; it is, "so to speak, *doubly integrated*. The Christian symbols affect their own patterning of a life which receives them, and the poet adds his own further shaping as he incorporates them into his closely unified poem."[13]

One must allow, certainly, that this is a possible view to take of the purposes of poetry in general and of religious poetry in particular; and I shall be suggesting promptly that it has relevance to the poets who are the subject of this study. It stands in striking contrast, however, to the injunctions against simplification and manipulation which constitute the main faith of the realistic novel, and it finds no support in the major formulations of modern critical theory, or in the discussion of the metaphysical poets, who have provided some of the chief touchstones for that theory. It is contradicted absolutely in some important theoretical pronouncements. I. A.

13. Ibid., pp. 88, 139.

Richards, for example, calls for a poetry of "inclusion," making use of no "suppressions and sublimations" to reduce the stress of complexity and contradiction in life, but achieving "repose *in the midst of stress,*" a balance in which the opposing impulses retain their vitality undiminished.[14] For Richards this is a process especially characteristic of tragedy, which is "the greatest and rarest thing in literature." But a poetry which avoids suppressing the opposites of experience would seem self-evidently to be one which is cautious in its use of poetic techniques of integration and distrustful of the doctrines of integration which religion makes available.

In Richards's view, one imagines, a doubly integrated poem (the religious poem per se, according to Hepburn) would be a doubly bad one. Tragedy, literature's supreme achievement, says Richards, "is only possible to a mind which is for the moment agnostic or Manichean. The least touch of any theology which has a compensating Heaven to offer the tragic hero is fatal."[15] Murray Krieger, perhaps the most resolute upholder of opposites in poetry, renews Richards's argument for the necessity of an agnostic or Manichean metaphysical outlook to support poetic opposites, drawing the lines even more sharply which would cut off the (religious) integrations of doctrine and the (literary) doctrines of integration from the work of literature. His discussion of poetic meaning outlines a "literary discipline" to which he gives the name "thematics"—a study which finds its objects in the existential opposites of the world view reflected in the literary work.[16] As a "discipline" or "method," it has perplexingly the look of a mere *proposition;* that is, simply that the world view reflected in a

14. *Principles of Literary Criticism* (London, 1925), p. 246.
15. Ibid.
16. *The Tragic Vision: Variations on a Theme in Literary Interpretation* (New York, 1960), pp. 241–42.

literary work must necessarily be bipolar and tensional. It is a proposition which deserves attention in the present context, however, to the extent that it illuminates the ways in which attitudes indigenous to modern realism have entered poetic theory and become confused with the attitudes of seventeenth-century poets, whose work supplied many of the justifying examples with which the theorists began. Thematics, says Krieger,

> as the only method capable of dealing with meanings in literature, would seem to predispose the moral-theological—indeed finally the metaphysical—issue toward the irresolution of Manichaeism. It would seem to argue against any cosmic resolution, however ultimate and however qualified, since this would reduce the complexities of the theme . . . to the single-mindedness of "philosophy" and thus reduce poetry to its "Platonic" conception as a form of propositional discourse.[17]

So firmly is Krieger's face set against such extrapoetic integrations as those envisaged in Hepburn's (d) that he declares for the view that "what literature is for" is to make revelations about "the befuddling nature of existence."[18] His use of the word "Manichean"—picked up,

17. Ibid., p. 243.
18. Ibid. W. K. Wimsatt has argued against such "didacticism" in the theory of oppositional poetics while upholding opposition as an essential principle of aesthetic autonomy—a position which finds ground for the poetry of opposites independent of modern realism, but which does not suggest a more appropriate context of attitudes for the oppositional poets of the seventeenth century. Wimsatt's argument for the *necessity* of opposites merits citing, however, in illustration of the modern critic's attachment to this theory of poetic structure.

> The principle of conflict, for the poet . . . is one that has to be lived with, deeply. For the critic too and the literary theorist, it is one that has to be lived with. . . . this saving

evidently, from Richards—appears to be casual and not intended to bear much literal weight. It is not merely mischievous, however, to point out that to the poets of the English seventeenth century whose practices in poetry have, willy-nilly, stimulated this vein of theorizing Kriegers' irresolvable opposites were not visible, and Manichaeism was a name for a particularly repugnant heresy, a denial of the sovereignty of God, by no means reconcilable with their Christian faith. The notion is the more remarkable, of course, as it applies to the first part of the century, when idiosyncratic private and sectarian theologies were not uncontrolled, and poets worshiped in the church. Even later (as with Milton) their devotion to existential opposites would seem not to have been of the sort that recent criticism would like to find, and it will be the business of pages following to show the extent of their "exclusiveness" in Richards's sense: their "suppressions" and "sublimations" and "subversions," their various devices of retreat from the confrontation standardly enjoined upon the modern (and originally, it seems clear, the modern novelist) to "find truth" by "seeing life without rearrangements" and giving full play to its contradictions.

My object will be to identify, on the basis of a historical and intellectual background remote from the background

---

principle of opposition . . . a principle which embraces the logic of metaphor, the drama of action, the psychology and the ethics of doubt and irony. After the dialectic of the various other sorts of poetic has run its course—after the claim for scientific, philosophic or religious truths of content has been stated, and response, and after all merely formal claims of structure, texture, style or technique—the special formality of the tensions, elusive and treacherous as it may be, seems to be the surviving cognitive principle. ["Horses of Wrath: Recent Critical Lessons," *Essays in Criticism*, 12 (1962): 1–17].

of modern realism, the opposites which engaged the imaginations of seventeenth-century poets and to describe
the characteristic interaction of these opposites in their
poems. The background to be cited will suggest the term
"Augustinian" as an alternative to "Manichean," and the
pattern of interaction described (in which conflicts appear
to be contrived only to end in resolutions) will suggest
that "poetry of reconciliation" comes nearer than "poetry
of opposites" to the emphasis intended by seventeenth-
century poets.

One proposes a benefit beyond the clarification of
terms and improved understanding of exemplary poems.
It is that of proving a measure of coherence on a major
period in literary history which has seemed disjoint. In
the standard treatment of the period, the seventeenth
century begins "metaphysical" and ends "Augustan,"
with Milton not assimilated to either kind. There is no
question, of course, that these standard categories are
useful and reflect real facts of the literary situation, but
when one finds students of the period remarking its
tendency to "slide apart like a pack of tapered cards,"[19]
it may be questioned whether the mutual exclusiveness
of "metaphysical" and "Augustan" has not been exag-
erated; and the failure of these categories to accom-
modate a poet of Milton's importance is striking evidence
that they do not classify the period exhaustively. The
need to supplement them and reduce their mutual isolation is recognized implicitly in a number of studies which
have attempted to make use of style concepts and categories borrowed from art history, notably Mannerism and
baroque. But the difficulty of proving credible parallels
between English poetic styles and European art styles
which had very little chance to establish themselves in

19. Roy Daniells, "Baroque Form in English Literature," *University of Toronto Quarterly*, 14 (1944–45): 407.

England has caused these attempted importations to be
met with distrust. There will be occasion in the present
study, also, to refer to developments in European art, but
such references have been kept to a minimum and are
intended, not to prove an English baroque or Mannerism, but to illustrate the scale of a momentous event in
intellectual history—the revival in the Reformation
period of a theological position and certain general
attitudes associated with it first fully articulated in the
writings of St. Augustine—in which England and English
poets (metaphysicals and Milton alike) variously shared.

That an "Augustinian revival" did occur in the sixteenth and seventeenth centuries and that it has relevance to the study of seventeenth-century English poetry
is not, of course, a proposition in need of proving. The
renewal of Augustine's influence is authoritatively discussed in such familiar and respected works in the history
of ideas as Perry Miller's *New England Mind* and Herschel Baker's *The Wars of Truth;* and Louis Martz, in
The Paradise Within, has traced an important theme in
Augustine through works of Traherne, Vaughan, and
Milton.[20] The intended contribution of the present

20. Perry Miller, *The New England Mind* (New York, 1939);
Herschel Baker, *The Wars of Truth: Studies in the Decay of Humanism in the Earlier Seventeenth Century* (Cambridge, Mass.,
1952); Louis L. Martz, *The Paradise Within: Studies in Vaughan,
Traherne and Milton* (New Haven, 1964). Martz discusses a more
Platonic and optimistic side of Augustine than appears in the
present study, an Augustine who concedes some spiritual power to
man and conceives of spiritual life as a search for the Image of God
in the human soul. I have treated mainly the Augustine of the
Reformation, the sponsoring philosopher of the doctrines of human
depravity and divine grace and a principal figure in the history of
religious conversion. The contradictions are those of superabun-
dance, and it deserves bearing in mind that among Augustine's traditional titles is not only "Doctor of Grace" but "Doctor of All the
Churches."

study is to suggest a relation between the Augustinian
revival and the structure and form of poems. To an
extent, it will try putting poetic theory to school to
history, adjusting the "poetics of opposites" to square
with the imperatives of a historical situation in which
the oppositions most certain to engage poets' imaginations
were the theological oppositions which the great energies
of the Reformation found waiting for revival in Augustine.

1   A Pattern of Contraries

The feature of seventeenth-century metaphysical poetry to which Richards's and Krieger's use of the term "Manichean" points is its dialectical mood and process, an urgency and thoroughness of argument which makes room for the interaction of opposing impulses and attitudes and which, in many poems, utilizes the conflict of metaphysical categories: time and eternity, divine nature and human nature, multiplicity (or duality) and unity.[1] This tendency is kept from being Manichean in any

1. James Smith's well-known essay "On Metaphysical Poetry" (cited above) has been helpful in making these identifications. My differences from Smith are considerable, however, and it will perhaps be useful to state them fully. Smith values Donne as the possessor of a metaphysical imagination of the kind characteristic of "the great metaphysicians" and compares him especially with Thomas Aquinas. This imagination explains some particular features of Donne's poetry, such as its concern with problems related to "the problem of the many and the one" and a certain equivocation in its conclusions. For it is typical of great metaphysicians that "in their work there is the pursuit rather than the attainment of truth; and such value as their work possesses seems to depend wholly on the pursuit." The lack of certainty in metaphysical conclusions leads one kind of metaphysical intelligence to a special metaphysical excitement, accessible to the "few who, aware of the difficulty of metaphysical problems, see them lurking behind any action, however trivial, they propose. Such people will be in a state of great disturbance or at least excitement. Such excitement may well be an impulse to poetry, and the poetry it generates be metaphysical." There seems no reason to take issue with Smith's account of

theological sense, by its total neglect of what might be called the essential Manichean conceit—the notion of a polarization on a supernatural level of good and evil and the independent status of evil as an absolute principle. English seventeenth-century poets, until Milton, are notably unpreoccupied with supernatural evil, and Satan does not figure in *Paradise Lost* or *Paradise Regained* in such a way as to have tempted students of Milton to include Manichaeism among his heresies. Theologically, Donne is explicitly hostile to the central conceptions of Manichaeism and repeatedly takes occasion to state the orthodox alternatives. In his paraphrase of the "Lamentations of Jeremy," for example, he repeats the scriptural question and answer:

> Who then will say, that ought doth come to passe,
> But that which by the Lord commanded was?
> Both good and evill from his mouth proceeds.[2]

---

what metaphysicians think about and the sensations it may raise in them, nor to question the possibility that poetry "metaphysical" in his sense can be written. I do, however, question the applicability of Smith's description to his chosen English metaphysical poets— Donne, Herbert, and Marvell—poets distinguished, in his view, by a metaphysical awareness and excitement not present in Dante and Lucretius, who are merely the disciples of metaphysicians, not true metaphysicians themselves. The suggestion of my study is that, rather than reflecting the poet's personal powers as metaphysicians, the intensity of attention in seventeenth-century English poetry to the problems Smith calls metaphysical is a response to the prevailing Augustinian theology of the time, which gave almost obsessional urgency to the question of man's relation to God and which, in its peculiar antirationalism, precluded certainties as effectively as original speculation in metaphysics. The "excitement" or "disturbance" in the poems, I shall be trying to show, have a dogmatic basis in the theology of the Reformation.

2. *The Divine Poems of John Donne,* ed. Helen Gardner (Oxford, 1952), p. 43.

The philosophical attitudes most commonly identified
in metaphysical poetry seem to have no necessary connection with "Manichean" form, except as the clash and
interplay of metaphysical opposites may, perhaps, tend
naturally to the diminution of the human. (The human
is not merely diminished but labeled evil in the original
Manichean teachings. Adam was the child of Satan en-
gendered by Sin.) Certainly a kind of pessimism and antihumanism sounds stridently in many metaphysical poems
and has been often remarked: man is after all a tragically
limited creature, as they sometimes triumphantly, sometimes sadly, remind us.

> Poore soule, in this thy flesh what dost thou know?
> .   .   .   .
> Thou art too narrow, wretch, to comprehend
> Even thy selfe.[3]

The fault lies often with reason. Indeed, a theme of
antirationalism, offering medieval wormwood to human
pride and self-content, is perhaps the most interesting
feature of the movement now familiarly identified as the
"Counter-Renaissance." The basis upon which the entire
structure of Renaissance education and morality had
been founded was the notion of man's essential ration-
ality. Ethics, in the Renaissance conception, could not
be written on any other supposition, and that supposition was made axiomatic by an immense weight of
authority. "Rational creature" had been for Aristotle a
sufficient definition of man,[4] and it sufficed the Renaissance generations for most intellectual purposes. Text-
books in logic, for example, employed the rational defini-

3. John Donne, *The Anniversaries,* ed. Frank Manly (Baltimore,
1963).
4. *Nichomachean Ethics,* 1098[a]13-14.

tion of man—*Homo est animal rationale*—as a standard example of essential definition.[5]

Objections to and qualifications of this definition become a familiar theme of seventeenth-century reaction, assisted in its attack by the more penetrating psychology of the new age. *Nosce teipsum* was a challenge accepted by some surprising literalists, whose self-examinations did not support Aristotle's rational ethics and psychology. Montaigne's satisfied account of himself, for example, would make him a case of moral pathology in Aristotle's terms (something approaching the condition of the "incontinent man," whose characteristic is to know the good but to be unable to follow it), and his notorious opinion, in the *Apology for Raimond Sebond,* that man is scarcely, on the score of reason, to be distinguished from the brutes, flies directly in the face of the conventional—and Aristotelian—wisdom of the Renaissance.

Sir Thomas Browne's critique of reason (or random antirationalism) is more explicitly anti-Aristotelian: *"Aristotle,* whilst hee labours to refute the Idea's of Plato, fals upon one himselfe; for his *summum bonum* is a Chimaera, and there is no such thing as his Felicity. That wherein God himselfe is happy, the holy Angels are happy, in whose defect the Devils are unhappy, that dare I call happinesse."[6] For Aristotle, and for Renaissance humanism, happiness had been a condition possible under the sun. It belonged not to gods or angels but

5. R. S. Crane, "The Houyhnhnms, the Yahoos and the History of Ideas," *Reason and the Imagination: Studies in the History of Ideas, 1600–1800,* ed. J. A. Mazzeo (New York, 1962), p. 239. Crane shows that this definition of man's essence was an "omnipresent" truism in the logic text books.

6. *Religio Medici,* ed. L. C. Martin (Oxford, 1964), Part II, Sec. 15.

exclusively to man and was inseparable from his rational
faculty. As the human "highest good," the attainment of
happiness was the "end" for which the defining human
"function" of reason was most appropriately employed.

John Marston is another who takes his antirationalism
to Aristotle: even the best man, he says,

> . . . hath no soule the which the Stagerite
> Term'd rationall: for beastly appetite,
> Base dunghill thoughts, and sensuall action,
> Hath made him loose that faire creation.
> And now no man, since *Circe's* magick charme
> Hath turn'd him to a maggot that doth swarme
> In tainted flesh, whose foule corruption
> Is his fayre foode: whose generation
> Anothers ruine.[7]

Dunghill thoughts and beastly appetite speak in some
of the poems of *Songs and Sonnets* and in the secular
lyrics of other metaphysicals and their imitators among
the Cavalier and Restoration poets. Donne, in this vein,
asks to be recognized as one of the "advanced" con-
fronters of the truth of man's animal nature, and there
is, to be sure, a good deal in such a program that seems
to match the purposes of modern realism. His "anti-
Petrarchan" poems, exploding idealisms, make a joke of
the Elizabethan Petrarchists' aesthetically ordered world
purified of gross passions, in which the devotions of lovers
resemble religious devotions and in which a mistress,
typically, is a gentle Diana. Donne's alternative to this
world and to the people who inhabit it is consistent with
the seventeenth-century challenge to Renaissance notions
of the nature of man. Human passion in such a poem
as "The Apparition" is scarcely distinguishable from

7. "The Scourge of Villainy," vii.66–74, *The Poems of John
Marston*, ed. Arnold Davenport (Liverpool, 1961), p. 142.

animal appetite: physical description changes from the Elizabethans' ideal abstraction to the brutal circumstantiality of "a cold quicksilver sweat" in an enseamed bed.

Donne's realism in this kind of exercise does not exhaust his attitudes, however, and would seem in its headlongness to lack the characteristics essential to the opposition-structured, or "Manichean," poem described in recent criticism and hallowed in current critical theory. We see no evidence of an intention "to be just to the complexity of experience" by maintaining a scrupulous balance among alternatives and contradictions. And if there is an impression of conflict, it is evidently not the kind of conflict which arises as the result of a dialectical play of opposite impulses, but the simpler conflict of a mind in real or pretended disagreement with its world and expressing itself unrestrainedly: "Oh, 'tis imposture all."

It would seem possible to argue that Donne is most Manichean, or makes most display of his supposedly Manichean and agnostic formal qualities, in his explicitly Christian poems. This makes a puzzle of considerable difficulty, and, of course, suggests a need for clearer understanding of the relations between poetry and religion in the period. Without pausing to refer to contexts and traditions which will be discussed later, one can perhaps make some initial progress with a bald statement of certain propositions bearing on the problem. It seems useful, in short, to maintain (1) that although human nature is desperately limited in Donne's conception, that circumstance is not conclusive for human possibility; (2) that the opposites of metaphysical poetic strategy are related to a theological conception of reality which has extremely few points of contact with agnostic-ism or Manichaeism (certainly no more contact than can be claimed for a traditional strain of Christian dualism); (3) that the opposition of opposites in seventeenth-century poetry is not absolute as the term would be understood in metaphysics: the world and man, rather than an independent energy of evil, provide the counterweight to God, and they are of course God's own creations—evil only insofar as they withdraw from him; (4) that the structural purpose of opposition in the poems lies not in dialectic interplay for its own rewards but, rather, in the reconciliation in which it concludes—a reconciliation which the inequality of the opposed forces makes inevitable from the outset.

Given the last point, there would seem to be an advantage in accuracy in replacing the notion of "poetry of opposites" with "poetry of reconciliation" in our approaches to the seventeenth century. Man's determination to go one way is negated by God's determination that he shall go another, and the decisiveness in the poems of God's determination is a dramatization of his reconciling power. This point is not contradicted by the vigor of human assertiveness in the poems, which discovers itself in the end to be both doctrinally justified and a necessity of dialectic strategy. The assertion, the almost antic busyness of human will, gives a challenge to the divine power to bring quiet ("Thou hast us for thyself, O Lord," wrote St. Augustine, "and our hearts are restless until they rest in thee"), and the power to bring quiet manifests itself in response. The end of Herbert's poem *The Collar* is perhaps the clearest possible example: "Me thoughts I heard one calling, *Child!* / And I reply'd, *My Lord.*"

Motion and countermotion are parts of a mechanism designed to bring on reconciliation—characteristically one of two types of reconciliation described by Ronald

W. Hepburn as among four types theoretically possible in poetry.[8] One of these, it will be recalled, is a resolution of tensions resulting from the introduction of new information which establishes decisively that one of a pair of alternative attitudes is the right one and the other wrong: God enters as a new and unexpected fact, and the speaker in Herbert's poem ceases to repine at the thanklessness of God's service. Clearly the opposites were not equal, and the poem has been committed from the first to a version of "truth" which would require the subordination of one term in the dialectic to the other. The other type in Hepburn's list that seems to describe the practice of the metaphysicals is reconciliation by appeal to a *doctrine of reconciliation*. The poet, in a religious poem, may in effect simply declare an end to the oppositions in the poem by drawing on the reconciling power of his religion—again a strategy perhaps only intelligible if the *sense of reconciliation* is the end being sought. Donne proceeds in this way, stanza by stanza in "Hymne to God My God in My Sicknesse," the last line of the poem summing up the reconciling sense of last lines of earlier stanzas: "Therefore that he may raise the Lord throws down." Both types of reconciliation are in a sense extra-poetic—both draw matter from outside the poem to aid in eliminating a condition represented inside it, ignoring what would appear to be the normal development of the "givens" of the situation with which the poem starts.

The "poetic" alternative to such reconciliations, as understood, for example, by Krieger or Richards, would involve neither additions nor eliminations and, in its most acceptable form, would leave the conflict of op-

8. See the Introduction above, n. 12, and Hepburn's (a) and (d), discussed in the text.

posites "not solved but only made manageable, control-
lable, by seeing it honestly as it is." The distinction is
similar to Richards's contrast of kinds of poetry "which
win stability and order through a narrowing of the
response (poetry of exclusion) with those that widen it
(poetry of inclusion)."[9] There is a sense in which one
can say that metaphysical poetry is poetry of exclusion
trying to look like poetry of inclusion.

A reading of Donne's "Goodfriday, 1613. Riding Westward" will illustrate the point. While appearing to suggest that more than one kind of attitude toward the
claims of the devout life is possible, in the end the poem
reveals itself as single-minded exposition of an orthodox
point of view. Its ostensible dualism is confined within
the limits of a ready-made stabilizing and unifying ap-
paratus of belief.

> Let mans Soule be a Spheare, and then, in this,
> The intelligence that moves, devotion is,
> And as the other Spheares, by being growne
> Subject to forraigne motions, lose their owne,
> And being by others hurried every day,
> Scarce in a yeare their naturall forme obey:
> Pleasure or businesse, so, our Soules admit
> For their first mover, and are whirld by it.
> Hence is't, that I am carryed towards the West
> This day, when my Soules forme bends toward the
>   East.
> There I should see a Sunne, by rising set,
> And by that setting endlesse day beget;
> But that Christ on this Crosse, did rise and fall,

9. I. A. Richards, *Principles of Literary Criticism* (London,
1925), p. 248.

Sinne had eternally benighted all.
Yet dare I'almost be glad, I do not see
That spectacle of too much weight for mee.
Who sees Gods face, that is selfe life, must dye;
What a death were it then to see God dye?
It made his owne Lieutenant Nature shrinke,
It made his footstoole crack, and the Sunne winke.
Could I behold those hands which span the Poles,
And tune all spheares at once, peirc'd with those
    holes?
Could I behold that endlesse height which is
Zenith to us, and to'our Antipodes,
Humbled below us? or that blood which is
The seat of all our Soules, if not of his,
Make durt of dust, or that flesh which was worne
By God, for his apparell, rag'd, and torne?
If on these things I durst not look, durst I
Upon his miserable mother cast mine eye,
Who was Gods partner here, and furnish'd thus
Halfe of that Sacrifice, which ransom'd us?
Though these things, as I ride, be from mine eye,
They'are present yet unto my memory,
For that looks towards them; and thou look'st
    towards mee,
O Saviour, as thou hang'st upon the tree;
I turne my backe to thee, but to receive
Corrections, till thy mercies bid thee leave.
O thinke mee worth thine anger, punish mee,
Burne off my rusts, and my deformity,
Restore thine Image, so much, by thy grace,
That thou may'st know mee, and I'll turne my face.[10]

The tension of opposites in this poem is more talked

10. *The Divine Poems of John Donne*, pp. 30–31.

about in it than actual and present. Although eastward-
and westward-going are unquestionably real alternatives,
God's way and the world's way, there is not much felt
urgency to the world's way as the poem develops, no insistence on its independent claims (which, indeed, are
scarcely suggested). The westward-goer knows he should
be going east, but he attempts an evasion by imagining
himself unequal to the original Good Friday scene and
at the end of the poem turns his westward way into an
alternate route east: "I turne my backe to thee, but to
receive / Corrections, till thy mercies bid thee leave."

An appearance of argument, of balanced alternative
possibilities, is nonetheless maintained. The poem begins
almost in the manner of academic disputation—*setting*
the question: "Let man's Soule be a Spheare, and then . . ."
The sphere/soul analogy is then justified with an elaborate analytic-looking "then . . . so" explanation, which
takes us up to the passage of rapid-fire Good Friday
paradoxes. These, similarly, have an air of argument
without truly being such. They are closely packed and
energetic, and they reverse swiftly. Christ—the Sunne—
rises, i.e. mounts the cross, in order to set, or die. Con-
versely, he sets in order to rise, and by setting, the act
of sacrifice for man, achieves eternal life for man—an
"endlesse day" to prevent the endless night of sin. The
passage that follows—lines 15 to 34—also depends to some
extent on the play of paradox for its appearance of argument: the pathos of God's human misery in the Crucifixion
contrasted with the awfulness of his divine might—"those
hands which span the Poles, / And tune all Spheares
at once, peirc'd with those holes." Equally effective in
creating the dialectic illusion in this passage is the series
of rhetorical questions: "What a death were it then to see
God dye?" "Could I behold those hands?" "Could I behold

that endlesse height?" "Durst I upon his miserable mother cast mine eye?"

But there is no debate. The poem is *about* the inevitable dialogue between "the resolved soul and created pleasure," but that dialogue is scarcely part of the process of the poem. Even what would seem to be the grammatical necessities of such a dialogue are absent, as a few lines from Marvell's later contribution to this specialized genre will help to show. In Marvell's poem, Soul and Pleasure speak, for the most part, simple declarative sentences. The mood of verbs is indicative and the tense is present.

Pleasure
Welcome the Creations Guest,
Lord of Earth, and Heavens Heir,
Lay aside that Warlike Crest,
And of Nature's banquet share:
Where the Souls of fruits and flow'rs
Stand prepar'd to heighten yours.

Soul
I sup above, and cannot stay
To bait so long upon the way.

I do not suggest that Marvell's poem is not as fully in the reconciling mode as Donne's—its last lines make its affinities clear—but it manages to look more authentically dialectical than Donne's, partly by using the direct language of assertion and counterassertion.

"Riding Westward" also makes assertions ("But that Christ on this Crosse, did rise and fall, / Sinne had eternally benighted all"), but they are assertions contained, through the first thirty-four lines of the poem, in the subjunctive mood. Up to its closing passage, the poem is entirely in the spirit of "let's imagine"; it proposes responses to conditional situations; the apparent give-

and-take of assertion is really a revery among possibilities, set up in part by the rhetorical questions. One can say then that the tension of opposites in this part of the poem is not a real tension, that there is nothing at issue. There is, however, as we have seen, a turmoil that looks like tension, built up of paradoxes, questions, and assertions and the stresses of the debate that the poem is *about*. But turmoil will serve as well as tension as a pretext for reconciliation, and in "Riding Westward" that pretext is acted upon with thoroughness and efficiency.

The movement to reconciliation is marked by a general change in the strategy of the poem from description to dramatization, which is also, in grammatical terms, a change from subjunctive to indicative, from conditional to actual. God has been present only in the third person through the first thirty-four lines of the poem; he has been somewhat masked by metaphor (Sunne), and he has been imagined in abstract hugeness and omnipotence—"that endlesse height which is Zenith to us, and to'our Antipodes." He enters the poem immediately and over-whelmingly when he is suddenly addressed as "thou" in line 35.[11] The "let's imagine" abstractness earlier in the poem, the tentativeness of the rhetorical questions, gives way to an urgency of direct address: pronouns become vocatives and verbs imperatives.

> . . . and thou look'st towards mee,
> O Saviour, as thou hang'st upon the tree;
> I turne my backe to thee, but to receive
> Corrections, till thy mercies bid thee leave.
> O think mee worth thine anger, punish mee,
> Burne off my rusts, and my deformity,

11. The process of the poem can also be described with Lowry Nelson's conception of the baroque exploitation of rhetorical situation, manipulating and interchanging the roles of audience and reader; see *Baroque Lyric Poetry* (New Haven, 1961), pp. 87–98.

Restore thine Image, so much, by thy grace,
That thou may'st know mee, and I'll turne my face.

The new drama brings not only a new role for God,
but a new role for the speaker. He has been heretofore
the principal actor in the poem: he has ridden westward
on his own westward-going impulse, and he has imagined
himself in contemplation of various scenes of divine
majesty and misery. In the last movement of the poem,
however, he submits himself passively to the reforming
and regenerating disciplines of a God not merely im-
manent but overwhelmingly immediate and attentive.

Readers seem always to have sensed a continuity between the Donne of the secular poems and the Donne
of the divine poems, about whom there still clings some
air of the erotic. John Chudleigh, for example, in his
1635 funeral elegy, saw as clearly as any modern that the
feeling with which Donne addressed God was not wholly
different from the feeling with which he had earlier addressed mistresses: "He kept his loves," wrote Chudleigh,
"but not his objects." The parallel may be extended to
include the insistence upon the perfect sufficiency of love's
world in both kinds of poem, the exploitation of all the
reconciling power that inheres in the idea of love.

Inevitably, for Donne, that exploitation makes use of
the physical senses, with the consequence that in his religious poems and the *Sermons* and *Devotions,* God is
presented in a character which the senses can grasp. He
is imagined humanly and visibly—with a decided emphasis, as William R. Mueller has said in a recent study
of the sermons, "on his existence rather than his essence
. . . on his activity in the world of man."[12] It should be
added that this imagining of the divine has an emphasis
typical of early Protestantism. There is none of the
Catholic interest in the personality of Christ, and the

12. *John Donne, Preacher* (Princeton, 1962), p. 247.

only "activity of God in the world of man" that is fully
considered is his activity in reconciliation and redemption. It is God thus imagined who is asked in "Riding
Westward" to "punish mee / Burne off my rusts, and my
deformity." He appears still more vividly in many passages of the sermons, controlled, however, by the same
conceptions of divine function.

> And as *Elisha* in raysing the *Shunamits* dead child,
> put his mouth upon the childs mouth, his eyes, and
> his hands, upon the hands, and eyes of the child; so
> when my crosses have carried mee up to my Saviours
> Crosse, I put my hands into his hands, and hang
> upon his nailes, I put mine eyes upon his, and wash
> off all my former unchast looks, and receive a sov-
> eraigne tincture, and a lively verdure, and a new
> life into my dead teares, from his teares. I put my
> mouth upon his mouth, and it is I that say, *My God,
> my God, why has thou forsaken me?* and it is I that
> recover againe, and say, *Into thy hands, O Lord, I
> commend my spirit.* Thus my afflictions are truly a
> crosse, when those afflictions doe truely crucifie me,
> and souple me, and mellow me, and knead me, and
> roll me out, to a conformity with Christ. It must be
> this *Crosse,* and then it must be *my crosse* that I must
> take up, Tollat suam.[13]

One may well feel unease with this, but in its intensity of
embrace and self-surrender it does with the self—the God-
subverting element in Man—only what the seventeenth-
century mode of reconciliation demands. And it gives to
God that aggressiveness in love which, with varying
urgency, consistently characterizes his activity as master
reconciler.

13. *The Sermons of John Donne,* vol. 2, ed. George R. Potter
and Evelyn M. Simpson (Berkeley, 1953–62), p. 300.

2 The Tradition of Grace

The thesis anticipated in this discussion thus far is that
seventeenth-century poets developed a kind of poetry
having features of antihumanism and antirationalism in
content and (in its own qualified way) dialectical or oppositional in structure, reflecting in each of these features
the influence of Reformation theology. A theology of opposites, I shall be claiming, lies behind the poetry of
opposites written by some important and representative
seventeenth-century poets and lent them its urgencies and
formulas of reconciliation.

In validating that claim, I shall be less concerned to
study theology than to define an ethos, but it is an ethos
exceptionally accessible to definition. For whereas there
are difficulties perhaps never to be surmounted in trying
to define the essential qualities of the "Renaissance" and
fix the time of its occurrence, or in fitting adequate concepts to the terms "baroque" or "Mannerist" or "modern,"
there is no such looseness of reference with the concept
Reformation, and any proposition having to do with
Reformation ideas can be tested conclusively against a

variety of sources of unchallenged authority. As a historical episode, it was perhaps uniquely self-conscious and
self-defining. It was also comprehensive, affecting European civilization on a scale and with a decisiveness probably not matched by any other single event after the
barbarian invasions of the fifth century. The student of
Reformation influences in the literature of the seventeenth century thus has advantages beyond the clearness
of outline of his subject matter. His subject is also a
pervasive force which can be expected to manifest itself
as an informing principle in a great variety of works of
the period and as an influence that can be looked for
everywhere. Certainly his situation compares very favor-
ably with that of the student of science in poetry, who is
able to record that Donne, for example, had a considerable curiosity about scientific developments in his time,
but can scarcely undertake to show that Donne's imagination was scientific in its fundamental impulses. Such
a claim would not be excessive, as I trust will appear, for
the influence of the Reformation on Donne's religious
poetry.

The course of the Reformation in England was, to be
sure, more complicated than in other Protestant countries. The Elizabethan church, as every school child
learns, was a compromise, and the *via media* that
eventually emerged as its ideal was in part a defense
against the radical reforming views of Calvin and Luther
and in part a defense against the revived militancy of
Catholicism. But the idea of defense does not recognize
the complexity of Elizabethan objectives, which included
a judicious taking from both sides as well as resistance
to them. It is clearly possible to argue that more was
admitted from the Reformers' side and that Englishmen
of the seventeenth century had fully absorbed Reformation teaching with respect to the nature of man, the

processes of justification, the operations of grace, the "foundation of faith." And to follow Reform teaching on these matters was to follow it in essentials. Remaining, of course, were some extremely troublesome questions of ecclesiastical polity, but even Hooker considered that episcopacy was a matter "indifferent" to faith, and while church government was the original and most exacerbated point of difference between the Church of England and the Calvinists, it did not prevent the mixing of allegiances —perhaps the most striking of which occurred among the prelates themselves, for it has been claimed that there was hardly one of the Elizabethan bishops who was not a Calvinist.[1] Eventually, lines became more clearly drawn, but, despite the vigor of the counterattack under Laud, increasing clarity meant increasing gains (until after the midcentury) for the ideas of continental Reform.

One may ask how this dominance of Reformation ideas bears on the shaping of sensibility in Donne, who was reared in the Church of Rome. A possible answer, of course, is that a Catholic living in England during the Calvinist ascendancy could hardly escape forming some acquaintance with these ideas. A more satisfactory answer, however, and one that leads to larger conclusions concerning the religious climate of seventeenth-century English poetry, can be found by considering a general European movement of piety in which Catholicism participated together with Protestantism (and which existed as a Catholic movement before the Reformation). This will also provide a perspective in which important doctrinal emphases uniting the Church of England to other branches of reform will stand out clearly.

1. H. R. McAdoo, *The Spirit of Anglicanism: A Survey of Anglican Theological Method in the Seventeenth Century* (New York, 1965), p. 5.

It will be more useful to characterize this movement
than to give its history in detail, though its characteristics
will need describing with some particularity for nontheological readers, and I shall walk where a more adept
would fly. It is a movement which has been discussed in
studies of religious and intellectual history under the
name of "Augustinian revival," although it has its roots
(as does Augustine) in St. Paul.[2] Its central themes are
suggested perhaps most clearly in Paul's Epistle to the
Galatians, to which Luther was to give prominence in
sixteenth-century theological writing. "I am wedded to
it," he once said at table, "it is my Katie von Bora."

There can be no mistaking what Augustine and the
Reformers found in Galatians: Augustine cites it regularly; we have full commentaries on it by both Luther and
Calvin; and its support of essential Reformation positions is self-evident. In this epistle, Paul admonishes a
congregation which is tempted to the error of reviving
the law, and he sorts out their alternatives along a clear
line of division: on the one side God, Spirit, Faith, Salvation; on the other Man, Flesh, Law, Damnation. The
essential point is that the Christian should accept Christ
as the agent of his salvation, and the only agent possible
for him. To hope for salvation under the law is to put
faith in the saving power of human effort, which in
Paul's view is a ridiculous blasphemy and denial of the
miracle of God's grace.

"But that no man is justified by the law in the sight of
God, it is evident: for 'The just shall live by faith.' And
the law is not of faith" (Gal. 3:11–12). In fact, the law
is ineffective even in controlling the flesh, which follows
its own impulses (for without the aid of the Spirit "ye
cannot do the things that ye would") into "adultery,

2. See Perry Miller, *The New England Mind*, and Herschel
Baker, *The Wars of Truth*.

fornication, uncleanness, lasciviousness, idolatry, witch-craft, hatred, variance, emulations, wrath, strife, seditions, heresies, envyings, murders, drunkenness, revellings, and such like" (Gal. 5:19–21). To live in the spirit, on the other hand, is to enjoy freedom from the struggle to ful-fill the law and escape the inevitable defeat; "The fruit of the Spirit is love, joy, peace, longsuffering, gentleness, goodness, faith, meekness, temperance," and this is ac-cessible to faith alone (Gal. 5:22–23). Law and the effort of work toward salvation are fruitless and irrelevant, as the law's demand of circumcision symbolizes: "For in Christ Jesus neither circumcision availeth any thing, nor uncircumcision, but a new creature" (Gal. 6:15): That Paul can offer himself as such a new creature enormously enhances his persuasiveness. He has lived in error, the zealous and vengeful servant of the law; his conversion, when the Lord "called me by his grace" compellingly dramatized the divine renovating power for future cen-turies of Christianity.

For Augustine, Paul was the pencil, *stylus dei,* through whom God had communicated truth to Augustine him-self, and Paul's dualism of Spirit and Flesh is schematized in Augustine's structure of the two cities, earthly and heavenly, which "have been formed by two loves: the earthly by the love of self, even to the contempt of God; the heavenly by the love of God, even to the contempt of self."[3] The grace which in Paul works to liberate the Christian from Hebrew law appears in Augustine to liberate the soul from sin. In both, the result of grace is freedom, transformation, and forgiveness;[4] and for both

3. *City of God,* trans. Marcus Dods (New York, 1950), 14.28.
4. This interest in felt results is cited by Adolf Harnack as characteristic of the emphasis on the "practical element" in re-ligion, which, he argues, Augustine "brought . . . to the front more than any previous Church Father" *(History of Dogma,* trans. Neil Buchanan and James Millar, vol. 5 [Boston, 1910], p. 100).

the obstacle to the spiritual life is located in human nature itself. Augustine mines Paul for quotations and devotes much energy to the explication of the Pauline text. Section 32 of the *Enchiridion,* for example, is *in toto* a glossing of Romans 9:16. "So then it is not of him that willeth nor of him that runneth, but of God that sheweth mercy." The "true interpretation" of Paul here, according to Augustine, is that every step of the process of man's salvation is taken by God—"the whole work belongs to God, who both makes the will of man righteous, and thus prepares it for assistance, and assists it when it is prepared."[5] Now and then, as here, Paul anticipates Augustine's precision in locating the issue between God and man in will. Five of the epistles share an opening formula that calls attention to God's will as the source of Paul's own mandate ("Paul, an apostle of Jesus by the will of God . . . Unto the Church of God which is at . . ."), and the suggestion occurs repeatedly that it is simple perverseness, misdirection of the will, for man to follow the flesh: "But to Israel he saith, 'All day long I have stretched forth my hands unto a disobedient and gainsaying people' " (Rom. 10:21).

Such a view of man and man's relation to God provides the central pillars of Augustine's theology, thoroughly restored at the Reformation, and the structure of his vivid spiritual autobiography—an account of a confused struggle and flight from God until stunningly overtaken. For Augustine, man is benighted, besotted, and incompetent to achieve the only end that is appropriate to him—the saving knowledge and love of God. He is not without the faculty of reason, to be sure, and is capable of reaching a qualified kind of happiness in his attempt to live a good life, but "such peace as can be enjoyed in a

5. *The Enchiridion on Faith, Hope and Love,* ed. Henri Paolucci (Chicago, 1961), p. 40.

good life" bears no comparison with the joys of heaven and, indeed, may be considered by comparison "mere misery."[6]

Left to himself man cannot escape evil. He is conceived in sin and persists in sin until the infection of his will is purged by grace; and the restoration of man's will to God and its alienation from himself is what the religious life, finally, is about. "And this Thy whole gift was," says Augustine in the hymn of praise which opens Book IX of the *Confessions,* "to nill what I willed, and to will what Thou willest." The reform of the will *is* the conquest of evil. For the evil that man knows is the independence of his will from God's and its pursuit of its own ends. The fall, in Augustine's conception, was the first corruption of the will, in which we continue. "And I enquired what iniquity was, and found it to be no substance, but the perversion of the will, turned aside from Thee, O God."[7]

But man is not abandoned, and, although helpless himself to close the gap which keeps him from his real felicity, is acted upon by the love of God, which comes as grace to the individual Christian and which was made manifest in history in the person of Christ.

> "The Word was made Flesh and dwelt among us." Through the Man Christ you go to the God Christ. . . . The Word which was far from you became Man in your midst. Where you are to abide, He is God; on your way thither He is Man. Christ himself is both the Way by which you go and the Haven toward which you make your way. Therefore, the "Word was made Flesh and dwelt among us.' "[8]

6. *City of God,* 19.10.

7. *City of God,* Everyman's Library (London, 1907), 13.14.

8. *St. Augustine: Sermons on the Liturgical Seasons,* trans. Sister Mary Sarah Muldowney, R.S.M. (New York, 1959), Sermon 261.7, p. 385.

We "ascend through Christ."[9] Such an ascension is not
possible through mere human virtue and cannot even
be desired by the unassisted human will. All initiatives
come from God.

> Thou wast walking in thy own ways a vagabond,
> straying through wooded places, through rugged
> places, torn in all thy limbs. Thou wast seeking a
> home . . . and thou didst not find it. . . . There came to
> thee the Way itself, and thou wast set therein. . . .
> Walk by Him, the Man, and thou comest to God.
> By Him thou goest, to Him thou goest. . . . I do not
> say to thee, seek the way. The way itself is come to
> thee; arise and walk.[10]

The vision of man helpless and errant and of God
distant but overwhelming in his solicitude, is, of course,
an orthodox Christian vision and can be found in every
period and setting in the history of Christianity. It is not
absent even from the rational theology of Aquinas, with
its Aristotelian assumptions concerning the rational nature
of man and the perspicuousness of the "book of nature"
to man's reason—its confidence that the data of cognition,
natural knowledge, leads to God. Differences of emphasis
are obvious, however, between theologies that declare the
value of reason, knowledge, and the works of man, and
those (the "theologies of opposites") which give their attention to will, faith, and divine grace. Of the latter,
Augustine was the great prototype, spawning vigorous
ectypes of various degrees of mutual resemblance in the
period of the Reformation. Luther (who began his career,
significantly, as an Augustinian monk), Calvin, Melanchthon, Zwingli, the English Puritans, the French Jan-

9. Ibid., Sermon 261.8.
10. *Enarrations on the Psalms* 70; *Sermon de Script, N.T.*, 141.4.

senists, and the Italian *spirituali* all testify to the energy
of a revived Augustinism. Clearly the spirit was not confined to the Protestant revolt. Impulses of spiritual renewal within the Church also derived from Augustine:
Ficino regularly cites Augustine as his chief religious
authority, and Petrarch's famous ascent of Mont Ventoux
concludes with an episode in which he appears to re-
enact the conversion scene from Augustine's *Confessions*
with the aid of the book itself.[11]

Petrarch's is one of innumerable imitations which illustrate the force of Augustine's example. Lives were
shaped in the imaginations of people who lived them
and in the imaginations of biographers (as in the case of
Walton's *Donne*) according to the pattern of the *Confessions*. And the Augustine of the *Confessions*, struggling with his sins of concupiscence and ambition and
intellectual pride until finally surprised by the gift of
faith, became, like St. Paul and Mary Magdalen (the
latter a heroine especially dear to Catholic piety), a favorite saint of an age which seems to have found an increasing attraction, as the sixteenth century passed into
the seventeenth, in lives conspicuous for their spiritual
contrasts and exemplifying the swift converting power
of divine grace. Even more than the author of *The City
of God*, historians of Christian thought have shown, it
was this Augustine, "the religious individual, recounting
the story of his own inward combat with sin, who was
rediscovered in the Renaissance period."[12] Certainly, in

11. Francesco Petrarca, "The Ascent of Mont Ventoux," trans.
Hans Nachod, in *The Renaissance Philosophy of Man*, ed. Ernst
Cassirer, Paul Oskar Kristeller, John Herman Randall, Jr. (Chicago,
1948), p. 44.

12. Daniel D. Williams, "The Significance of Saint Augustine
Today," in *A Companion to the Study of St. Augustine*, ed. Roy
W. Battenhouse (New York, 1955), p. 8.

the *Confessions,* Augustine provided brilliant texts for
some typical attitudes of the century and arranged them
in brilliant contrasts. He has vividly the sense of his own
evil—"how foul I was, how cursed and defiled, besotted
and ulcerous. And I beheld and stood aghast." But he
has just as vividly the sense of release from his deformities
and of his dearness to God and dependency on him.

> But this Thy Word, were little did it only command
> by speaking, and not go before in performing. This
> then I do in deed and word, this I do *under Thy
> wings;* in over great peril, were not my soul subdued
> unto Thee under Thy wings, and my infirmity
> known unto Thee. I am a little one, but my Father
> ever liveth, and my Guardian is *sufficient for me.*[13]

His analyses of spiritual states have great psychological
penetration, and it is possible to feel that in the power
and intensity of his introspection he goes beyond some
of the most celebrated examiners of the self in the later
age. One may judge, for example, that Robert Burton
and Sir Thomas Browne have a master in the author
of the following passage whom they have not excelled:

> Whence is this monstrousness? and to what end? The
> mind commands the body, and it obeys instantly;
> the mind commands itself, and is resisted. The mind
> commands the hand to be moved; and such readiness
> is there, that command is scarce distinct from obedi-
> ence. Yet the mind is mind, the hand is body. The
> mind commands the mind, its own self, to will, and
> yet it doth not. Whence this monstrousness? and to
> what end? It commands itself, I say, to will and
> would not command unless it willed, and what it

13. *Confessions,* trans. E. B. Pusey, Everyman's Library (London,
n.d.), p. 207.

commands is not done. But it willeth not entirely: therefore doth it not command entirely. For so far forth it commandeth, as it willeth: and, so far forth is the thing commanded not done, as it willeth not. For the will commandeth that there be a will; not another, but itself. But it doth not command entirely, therefore what it commandeth, is not. For were the will entire, it would not even command it to be, because it would already be. It is therefore no monstrousness partly to will, partly to nill, but a disease of the mind, that it doth not wholly rise, by truth up-borne, borne down by custom. And therefore are there two wills, for that one of them is not entire: and what the one lacketh, the other hath.[14]

As much as Burton or Browne, of course, one can feel that this is psychology in the vein of Hobbes, who came also to a conception of antithetical wills. To Augustine, such oppositions are as visible in the frame of the universe and in the relations of man and God as they are in the minds of men: conflict and dualism are inherent in both microcosm and macrocosm, and the gap is bridgeable in each case only by divine grace. The act by which God cures the human will of its ambivalence is the same act as that which ends the separation between himself and fallen and alienated man. Reformation piety, in reaction against the rational demystifications of Rome—both theological and institutional—seemed to demand exactly such a sense of separations and oppositions promising reconciliations. Ernst Cassirer has sketched the background of ideas which invited this reaction.

> Plotinus and Neo-Platonism tried to unite the funda-
> mental ideas of Platonic and Aristotelian thought;

14. Ibid., pp. 165–66.

but in fact, they succeeded only in producing an eclectic mixture. The Neo-Platonic system is dominated by the Platonic idea of "transcendence," i.e., by the absolute opposition between the intelligible and the sensible. The opposition is described completely in Platonic fashion and, indeed, in language even more emphatic than Plato had used. But by adopting the Aristotelian concept of development, the Neo-Platonists resolved the dialectical tension indispensable to the Platonic system. The Platonic category of transcendence and the Aristotelian category of development mate to produce the bastard concept of "emanation." The absolute remains as the super-finite, the super-one, and the super-being, pure in itself. Nevertheless, because of the super-abundance in it, the absolute overflows, and from this super-abundance it produces the multiformity of the universe, down to formless matter as the extreme limit of non-being. . . . The Christian Middle Ages adopted this premise and reshaped it to suit its own ends. It gained thereby the fundamental category of graduated mediation, which on the one hand allowed the integral existence of divine transcendence, and on the other hand mastered it, both theoretically and practically, with a hierarchy of concepts and of spiritual forces. Through the miracle of the ecclesiastical order of life and salvation, transcendence was now both recognized and conquered. In this miracle, the invisible had become visible, the inconceivable had become conceivable to man.[15]

The transcendent and inconceivable were restored with the Augustinian spirit, which somewhat fitfully revived in

15. Ernst Cassirer, *The Individual and the Cosmos in Renaissance Philosophy*, trans. Mario Domandi (Oxford, 1963), p. 18.

the early Renaissance and came to a second full fruition
in the Reformation, and God was put at a distance from
man which gave intensity to the sense of human peril in
isolation, but which also heightened the miraculousness
of God's interest in man, encouraging trust in and surrender to the resoluteness of divine love. Augustine conveys equally the wonder of it and sense of elation and
enlargement from the limits of the self, and the inescapable
precondition of misery in alienation from God. What one
can perhaps risk calling the baroque imagination of the
seventeenth century is thus supported and, indeed, in a
measure, led by Augustine to its giant oxymorons: its
vision of the human soul willing and unwilling its salvation; detestable even by its own weak lights, yet visited by
God's love; subject equally and inescapably to self-induced
desolations and God-induced consolations, with God,
simultaneously distant and near, withholding and giving,
judging and loving.

Augustine was, of course, immediately accessible to
seventeenth-century religious poets, and the age knew him
intimately. He "fills the whole century," as a modern
student has written of his influence in France: "All quote
him, make use of him, comment on him even when they
have scarcely read him. . . . We see him referred to everywhere, as supreme authority. . . . This ended by becoming an obsession: No one dared suggest any reservations
or criticisms: St. Augustine in all things is always right."[16]
   The cult of the Saint himself flourished somewhat less
spectacularly in Protestant countries, and in England the
most "Augustinian" religious group, the Puritans, tended
to insist on its independence from all traditional author-

16. Henri Marrou, *St. Augustine and His Influence through the
Ages*, trans. Patrick Hepburn-Scott (New York, 1957), pp. 169–70.

ities.[17] It is clear, nonetheless, that there occurred an
immense inflation of Augustine's reputation and influence in England as in the rest of Europe, during the
Renaissance and Reformation periods. Some two hundred
early editions of his writings (including many false at-
tributions) had been issued very soon after the invention
of printing. The *Short-Title Catalogue* shows forty-five
items in English before 1640, and the first great Latin
editions of the complete works had appeared before
1600. English preachers invoked his name less often than
his doctrines, but it is prominent, even so, in the widely
circulated sermons and treatises of the great clerics of
the time. Coverdale, in his *Confutation of Standish,* is
able to cite twelve major loci in Augustine for the doctrine of justification by faith.[18] For Thomas Becon, he is
a universal authority to be consulted on almost every
question of doctrinal interest from the inspiration of
the writers of the scriptures to the physical nature of the
inhabitants of heaven.[19] Archbishop Sandys is an almost
equally attentive Augustinian, especially prompt in cita-
tion when the task at hand is to define grace. ("It is called
grace because it is given gratis; freely and undeservedly
on our parts to whom it is given. . . . to us it is both
offered and exhibited by the voluntary and unprovoked
operation of the spirit.")[20] There is no slackening of

17. Cf. William Haller, *The Rise of Puritanism* (New York,
1938), p. 85: "Actually, the Puritan preachers, Calvinists though
they were in varying degrees, referred as often to St. Augustine as
to the author of the *Institutes* but were chary on principle of
citing any merely human authorities whatsoever."

18. "A Confutation of the Treatise of John Standish," in *Remains of Myles Coverdale, Bishop of Exeter,* ed. Rev. George Pear-
son, B.D. (Cambridge, 1846), p. 340.

19. *Works,* ed. J. Ayre, 3 vols. (Cambridge, 1844).

20. *The Sermons of Edwin Sandys, D.D.,* ed. Rev. John Ayre,
M.A. (Cambridge, 1841), pp. 144–45; 297–98.

appreciation as the seventeenth century begins. The great preachers cite him constantly, and Donne is perhaps the greatest Augustinian enthusiast in the history of English preaching.

It is a feature of the revival of his reputation that Augustine, certainly the most accomplished controversialist of the early Church, is given a prominent place in English religious controversy; Catholic and Protestant versions of the *Confessions* and the *City of God* vied for public attention, and Augustine's opinions were regularly cited on all sides of the disputes that agitated the period (serving, for example, both Hobbes and Bramhall). *A Worke of the Predestination of Saints Wrytten by the Famous Doctor S. Augustine Byshop of Carthage,* translated by Nycolas Lesse (1552) is an early use of an English translation of Augustine to beat the Papists, a purpose declared in a dedicatory epistle which has many parallels: "To the confusion therefore, and shame of thos detestable and shamles heretiques, and for the erudition of the rest of the people, which are unlerned and ease to be deceaved, I have brought thos workes into oure mother tounge that all men maye understonde them." But Augustine was not merely a Protestant saint, and Loyola was as eager to enlist him as Calvin. Richard Woodcoke's *A Godly and Learned Answer to a Lewd and Unlearned Pamphlet* (1608) illustrates the continuing power of Augustine's attractiveness to controversialists on opposing sides. The work is made up of alternating paragraphs of Woodcoke's answer (labeled "Protestant") and excerpts from a pamphlet to which it responds (labeled "Papist"). A good part of the issue between them is a matter of settling whose claim to Augustine is the stronger. One is compelled to recognize, finally, that Augustine's presence was pervasive for more than a century of English Reformation and that authors of every variety of opinion and

concerned with every variety of subject, including some
that were nontheological, would find their favorite pre-
cedents in him.

Augustine's contribution *in propria persona,* considerable as it was, to the intellectual circumstances of English
seventeenth-century poetry was less than the contribution
which he made through the continental Reformation. It
was Augustine in Luther and Calvin, not Augustine by
himself, who accomplished the overthrow of a legalist
and sacramental scholastic theology and replaced it, for
most of northern Europe, with a doctrine rigorously
centered on the forgiveness of sin and declaring that
almost nothing that is human, except sin, is relevant to
that forgiveness.

This is not to ignore differences. Augustine's deep involvement in Platonism before his baptism has been said
to explain his inclination to relate sin and redemption
to nonbeing and being, and he appears to understand
grace as an act by which God endows man with a new
nature (in a sense not fully anticipated in St. Paul's
"new creature") elevating him from one ontological level
to another, a stage closer to the perfect being of God.
These conceptions are absent from Luther's thinking,
which tends to philosophical simplicity—indeed, to anti-
philosophical simplicity—and which focuses with greater
intensity on the role of Christ. The main lines of continuity are clear, however, and there can be no suspicion
of overstatement in the view that Luther, and following
him the other Reformers, "accepted the system of
Augustine."[21]

The system, in simple, as we have seen, originates in

21. B. A. Gerrish, *Grace and Reason: A Study in the Theology
of Luther* (Oxford, 1962), p. 166.

the view that man is a creature ruined at the fall by an act of his rational will, which thereafter exists in "bondage" to the interests of the self and the world and can only be liberated by an undeserved act of divine grace. Its existence in bondage is imaged for Augustine in the "Earthly City," which is scarcely altered in Luther's "Earthly Kingdom," the essential feature of each community being its assertion of independence from the will of God. Neither is for this reason simply evil, for each has its own limited goods, e.g., private morals and social order. In the ultimate scheme of things, however, they represent misdirection vis-à-vis the purposes of God and therefore, in the end, misdirection with respect to the true purposes of man also. Headed aright, the faculties of the soul regard only salvation, and the promptings of the restricted self are, by a sufficiently familiar Christian paradox, self-defeating and alien impulses. We have seen it put so in Donne.

> Let mans Soule be a Spheare, and then, in this,
> The intelligence that moves, devotion is,
> And as the other Spheares, by being growne
> Subject to forraigne motions, lose their owne,
> And being by others hurried every day,
> Scarce in a yeare their naturall forme obey:
> Pleasure or businesse, so, our Soules admit
> For their first mover, and are whirld by it.

In its weakness and depletion after the fall, the soul is easily whirled away from its natural motion, and indeed can scarcely find it. The freedom of the will has been lost and with it the capacity of the soul to fulfill the function for which it was created. Its irresistible tendency away from its true good is only correctable by an irresistible grace which will "Burne off my rusts and my deformity / Restore thine Image, so much, by thy grace"—a process which marks the end of human striving and leaves God the only actor, bringing such a grace to man as is "suited to an entirely impotent nature, wholly controlling choice and action, and leading irresistibly to good."[22]

A conspicuous feature of the system is its derogation of reason. For Augustine and Luther, it is a corollary of their position concerning the free will of unfallen man that he fell through the exercise of conscious, deliberate, and rational choice. "Augustine is perfectly uncompromising in affirming that the choice of the worse is the act of the highest principle in man. . . . It is his rational will that chooses, and that is the very core and seat of his existence as person."[23] Reason in fallen man is the seat of his corruption. Luther makes his most famous attack on it in his last sermon (1546), calling it "the Devil's Whore," "beast," "enemy of God," "carnal," and "stupid."[24] Elsewhere he singles out Aristotle as reason's symbolic representative and abuses him as "the stinking philosopher," "the clown of the High Schools," "trickster," "rascal," "liar and knave," "the pagan beast," "blind pagan," "triple-headed Cerberus," "lazy-ass," "billy-goat."[25] The point is clear that reason is utterly disqualified for any mediating role between the lower faculties of man and the spiritual world; far from reducing the dualism of heavenly and earthly purposes, it bears the blame for man's original separation from God and for his continuing disposition to go his own way "even to the contempt of God."

But reason has a more ingratiating aspect which must

22. J. B. Mozely, *A Treatise on the Augustinian Doctrine of Predestination* (London, 1883), p. 154.

23. Robert Loury Calhoun, *Lectures on the History of Christian Doctrine* (New Haven, 1949), p. 216.

24. Gerrish, *Grace and Reason*, p. 1.

25. Ibid., p. 2.

also be resisted, for reason teaches ethics, and ethics teaches works, which is inimical to faith.

> Since human nature and natural reason, as it is called, are by nature superstitious and ready to imagine, when laws and works are prescribed, that righteousness must be obtained through laws and works; and further, since they are trained and confirmed in this opinion by the practice of all earthly law-givers, it is impossible that they should of themselves escape from the slavery of works and come to a knowledge of the freedom of faith.[26]

There is nothing to be objected to in the intentions of earthly lawgivers, whose value for works is appropriate in their sphere of operations. But it is vivid to Augustine and the Reformers that the sphere of the lawgivers (political society) belongs to the earthly kingdom—or city—and affords no means of approach to the heavenly kingdom. The dualism is complete: reason belongs to the flesh, and "nothing that belongs to the flesh can bring a man to God."[27]

Luther has been accused of indifference to morals, a charge which must in some measure be allowed against all of Augustine's theological progeny. All, to be sure, declare that the outer man should exist in conformity with the inner man reconstructed by grace, and all recognize that social virtues are necessary to social life. But their primary attention is given to the matter of salvation, and in that context they find morals not merely uninteresting, but dangerous. Every notion of human merit is an obstacle to faith. Mankind is "full of sin and a mass of perdition," and righteousness is hopelessly

26. Luther, "The Freedom of a Christian," in *Three Treatises,* trans. W. A. Lambert (Philadelphia, 1943), p. 315.

27. Gerrish, *Grace and Reason,* p. 71.

beyond its power to achieve. Indeed, mankind should not desire to achieve righteousness, for its helplessness in sin is what calls forth God's redeeming grace. "God wants sinners only," says Luther. "What connection could there be between abundant mercy and human holiness? If mercy is this abundant, then there is no holiness in us. Then it is a fictitious expression to speak of a 'holy man' . . . for by the nature of things, this cannot be."[28] To work for or claim diminished sinfulness is absurd. We "must learn from Paul" (Gal. 1:4) that

> Christ was given not for sham or counterfeit sins, not yet for small sins, but for great and huge sins; not for one or two sins but for all sins; not for sins that have been overcome . . . but for invincible sins. . . . Unless you are part of the company of those who say "our sins," that is, who have this doctrine of faith and who teach, hear, learn, love and believe it there is no salvation for you.[29]

The revolutionary scope of these doctrines in the sixteenth century can be estimated by a glance at contemporary Roman practice to which, in the Reformers' hands, they were a specific response. The very organization of the Church, for example, appears dedicated to the obliteration of the simple dualistic distinction that Augustine and Luther would have occupy the central place in devout imaginations. It assumes an order of merit in society at large—an order in which pride of place belongs to the clergy—and it distinguishes elaborately among clerical ranks. Luther, impatient of such pretensions—even the pope is only "a poor stinking

28. Luther's *Works,* vol. 12, *Psalms,* ed. Jaroslav Pelikan (St. Louis, 1955), pp. 324–25.

29. Luther's *Works,* vol. 26, *Lectures on Galatians,* ed. Jaroslav Pelikan (St. Louis, 1962), p. 35.

sinner"[30]—took arms against the system of works, rewards, and "powers" which supported them. But the
effort required almost a redefinition of religion. The
ancient sacraments of the Church were put under attack,
the priesthood challenged, the claims of the saints denied,
the conception of salvation as a reward for virtue treated
as a grotesque superstition. Every rung of the elaborately
contrived ladder by which the medieval Church had
sought to move man toward God is resolutely hacked
away. Church historians have seen the difference between
the conceptions in almost diagrammatic terms:

> Protestantism, in rejecting the pyramidal institution
> of Roman Catholicism, rejected also much of the
> pyramidal philosophy with which that institution
> was peculiarly associated. It put in the forefront of
> its concerns not synthesis but conflict, not the
> ordered sequence of elements in human nature but
> the antagonism between flesh and spirit. . . . It
> emphasized . . . not the harmony of God's universe
> but the infinitude of distinction which separated
> salvation from damnation. It emphasized sin.[31]

The Protestant emphasis on sin is not in itself
morbid or negative, however, and is not aimed at induc-
ing despair. Indeed, Augustine and the Reformers quite
explicitly offer their doctrine as a specific against hope-
lessness. To recognize man's inherent sinfulness is
to cease self-blame for failure to achieve righteousness
and to appreciate the immense generosity of the gift of
grace, God's infinite and self-giving *misericordia* for
man's dire *miseria*. Grace is an overwhelmingly larger

30. "An Open Letter to the Christian Nobility," in *Three
Treatises*, p. 58.
31. Charles H. George and Katherine George, *The Protestant
Mind of the English Reformation* (Princeton, 1961), p. 34.

gift in Augustinian-Protestant theology than in the
Thomist theology against which it reacted, and that
difference, too, is an aid in estimating the scope of
Luther's revolution. St. Thomas insists, to be sure, that
grace is necessary, that man cannot achieve salvation on
his own. Grace comes not to sinners, however, in the
Thomistic analysis, but to the virtuous, and is therefore
not the "efficacious" grace of Reformation theology, but
a grace that merely "assists" a process which is already
humanly begun and which must be humanly continued,
stage by stage, to final forgiveness.[32] Luther eliminates
both the human effort and the gradualism, substituting
the simple miracle described by Paul in which God does
all and does it "all at once" (ganz auff eyn mal).[33]

The essentials of the pattern are repeated in Calvin.
Once man is "covered with the righteousness of Christ"
there is no further forgiveness to be given, and justification is complete. Moreover, despite the darker implications of his doctrine of double predestination, Calvin no
less than Luther celebrates the "miraculous lenity" of
God's dealing with man and as consistently sounds the
theme of gratefulness for divine mercy. While man deserves destruction, he receives mercy instead, and such
mercy as God must exert himself to give. For "God finds
nothing in men which can incite him to bless them, but
that he prevents them by his gratuitous goodness." The
condemnation we have earned "is swallowed up by the
salvation of Christ."[34] God's inexplicable benevolence
passes all distances and overcomes all obstacles.

32. See Summa Theologica, q. 113, art. 1 ("Whether the Justification of the Ungodly Is the Remission of Sins?").

33. It deserves pointing out that the miraculousness of grace is
explicitly denied by Aquinas, q. 113.

34. Institutes of the Christian Religion, 7th American ed., trans.
John Allen (Philadelphia, 1936), 3.xiv.13; 3.xiv.5; 3.ii.24.

Calvin is no less explicit than Luther in avowing discipleship to Augustine,[35] seeing himself, in fact, as a second champion against the Pelagians,[36] and no less exact in stating the terms of the Augustinian dualism. Man's nature was wholly corrupted by Adam's act of will and continues in wilful corruption. "The blinding of the wicked and all those enormities which attend it are called the works of Satan, the cause of which must nevertheless be sought only in the human will, from which proceeds the root of evil, and in which rests the foundation of the kingdom of Satan, that is, sin."[37] For Calvin, as for the Reformation as a whole, sin is opposition to God: "We are enemies to God, and opposed to his righteousness in every affection of our heart" and nothing can close the "distance between the spiritual glory of the Speech of God and the abominable filth of our flesh"[38] except God's grace, which overthrows our wicked wills, converting us to God's direction and introducing us to the condition of reconciliation which the Reformation celebrated under the name of Christian liberty: "The primitive liberty was a power to abstain from sin, but . . . ours is much greater, being an inability to commit sin."[39] The process is analogous to a new creation of man, for, as we are before regeneration, "the life of God is extinguished in us," and we are, in a sense, dead.[40] Grace remakes us, displacing the old will

35. Calvin quotes Augustine more frequently than any other author. Leroy Nixon, *John Calvin's Teachings on Human Reason* (New York, 1963), p. 15, counts 228 quotations from Augustine, only 39 from Calvin's next-most-quoted author, Gregory I.

36. *Institutes,* 2.iii.13.

37. Ibid., 2.iv.1.

38. *Commentary on the Gospel According to John,* trans. William Pringle, reprint (Grand Rapids, 1956) 1:205–06, 1:45.

39. *Institutes,* 2.iii.13.

40. *Commentary,* 1:45.

and the old self with new instruments responsive to God. "For by the inspiration of his power he so breathes divine life into us that we are no longer actuated by ourselves, but are ruled by his action and prompting. Accordingly, whatever good things are in us are the fruits of his grace; and without him our gifts are darkness of mind and perversity of heart."[41]

Among the great Reformers, it is Calvin, of course, whose influence worked most strongly in the English Reformation and who can be held most directly responsible for the Augustinism of the Elizabethan church—as revealed, for example, in Articles IX through XVIII of the *Thirty-nine Articles of the Church of England,* which established as national belief the "corruption of the nature of euery man . . . whereby man . . . is of his owne nature inclined to euyll [and] deserueth God's wrath and damnation," prevenient grace, and justification "only for the merite of our Lord and sauior Jesus Christe, by faith, and not for our owne workes or deseruynges."[42] This is nothing more than a "plain transcript of S. Austin's Doctrine," as Bishop Burnet would complain at the beginning of the eighteenth century,[43] when the doctrine had become an embarrassment.

One might imagine that the necessity of subscribing to these articles would have given some discomfort to the "Arminian" party of Andrewes and Laud. Yet it is not clear that they were, in fact, seriously inconvenienced, or that the "Arminian" interest supposedly represented by them was in any important way anti-Calvinist or anti-Augustinian. Laud wrote the Royal Declaration which

41. *Institutes,* 3.i.3.

42. *The Creeds of Christendom,* ed. Philip Schaff (New York, 1877), 3:492–99.

43. Gilbert Burnet, *An Exposition of the Thirty-nine Articles* (London, 1699), p. i.

even now prefaces the *Thirty-nine Articles*. King James, under whose name it was given, was the abettor of Laudian reforms, but also the defender of Calvinism at the Synod of Dort. Andrewes, to be sure, attacked the extreme Calvinism of the Lambeth Articles issued by Archbishop Whitgift in 1595, but it is quite clearly an attack made from within the main positions of Reformation Augustinism. Andrewes objects to the idea that God condemned the reprobate to sin, but his objection merely aims at a clearer identification of the source of evil in the human will and a larger vision of divine grace, which would be conferred on all men but for the hardening of will in some.[44]

It is plain that the party in the English church which, as Trevor-Roper puts it, "regretted the thoroughness of the Reformation"[45] was not opposed to it root and branch. Even Hooker, whose *Laws of Ecclesiastical Polity* aims at undermining the essential dualism and miraculism of Reformation theology by its insistence upon a universal system of law and reason connecting the human and divine, perceives the dualism and respects the miracle. In *A Learned Discourse of Justification,* he writes in a familiar strain of Augustinism. The minds of men are darkened by the original corruption. Human merit is an absurd pretense. Suppose that only one completely good action of one completely good man would suffice to save mankind and you must accept mankind's destruction, for "do you think that this ranson . . . would be found among the sons of men? The best things we do have somewhat in them to be pardoned. How then can we

44. "Judgment of the Lambeth Articles," in *Minor Works*, ed. J. Bliss (London, 1846). The doctrine of "universal grace" was one of the original (Dutch) Arminian positions.

45. *Archbishop Laud*, 2d ed. (London, 1962), p. 27.

do anything meritorious and worthy to be rewarded?"[46]
With no hope of justification by his own effort or merit,
man must depend on faith and the miracle of divine
grace, and even a very great sinner

> him being found in Christ through faith, and having
> his sin in hatred through repentance; him God be-
> holdeth with a gracious eye, putteth away his sin by
> not imputing it, taketh quite away the punishment
> due thereunto, by pardoning it; and accepteth him
> in Jesus Christ, as perfectly righteous, as if he had
> fulfilled all that is commanded him in the law: shall
> I say more perfectly righteous than if himself had
> fulfilled the whole law.[47]

Later, Jeremy Taylor, who made a stand in other circumstances against radical Calvinism, tells the same tale:
man sins and God forgives. And Taylor, like Luther and
Augustine, delights to contemplate that forgiveness at its
greatest stretch, not merely overcoming the indifference
of Everyman, but conquering the energy of wilful depravity in a significant sinner: "God pardons the greatest
sinners, and hath left them upon record. . . . Such were
St. Paul, a persecutor, and St. Peter, that forswore his
master, *Mary Magdalen* with seven devils, the thief upon
the cross, Manassas an idolator, David a murderer and
adulterer, the Corinthian for incest."[48]
Donne's sermons illustrate with equal vividness that
the Anglican *via media* was not a way chosen to avoid
the main defining positions of the revived Augustinian
theology. A recent study of the sermons suggests that

46. This *Discourse* is printed with *Of the Laws of Ecclesiastical
Polity*, Everyman's Library (London, 1907), 1:23.
47. Ibid., 1:21.
48. "Miracles of the Divine Mercy," in *Discourses on Various
Subjects* (Boston, 1816), 2:540.

Donne's "preoccupation with sin is indeed the mark of a converted man."[49] Against the background we have been considering, however, it seems clear that there is no need to postulate a personal experience of conversion to account for Donne's interest in sin. The Reformation had made sin and redemption not merely the central but very nearly the sole concern of religion, and Donne does not go beyond his contemporaries—and certainly not beyond his reforming predecessors—in the eagerness of his attention to it. The Anglican sermon, typically, stays with this concern until rational theology takes on new life with the Cambridge Platonists, who later in the century become notable preachers of morals. This countermovement was, of course, ultimately to triumph and give its character to Anglicanism from the Restoration on, and its implications for sermon-writers are stated by Swift, who declares that "the two principal Branches of Preaching, are first to tell the People what is their Duty; and then to convince them that it is so."[50] But the Cambridge Platonists themselves are not much more disposed than Donne to desert the themes of sin and redemption in their sermons, and on occasion take them up (especially Culverwel) with a clear Calvinist emphasis. The theological options of the period were, in fact, rather narrowly limited.

Evelyn Simpson estimates that Donne refers to St. Augustine approximately seven hundred times in the 160

---

49. William R. Mueller, *John Donne: Preacher* (Princeton, 1962), p. 168. Mueller comments on the tendency of Walton's and Gosse's biographies to impose an Augustinian conversion pattern on Donne's life. Walton, in fact, describes Donne as a "second Augustine."

50. "A Letter to a Young Gentleman Lately Entered into Holy Orders," *Irish Tracts, 1720–1723, and Sermons,* ed. Louis Landa (Oxford, 1948), p. 70.

extant sermons, and she counts 271 references to St. Paul
in 34 sample sermons (as compared to 113 references to
the four Gospels).[51] It is overwhelmingly clear that St.
Augustine is Donne's most heavily used nonscriptural
source and that St. Paul is his favorite source in scripture. This pattern of preference in authorities could
probably be shown to be almost a standard Reformation
pattern and reflects the characteristic Reformation intensity of interest in the great Pauline and Augustinian
themes of man's sin, God's mercy, and the process by
which mercy acts on sin.

To be sure, Donne insists on his differences with English
Calvinists. He despises the crude spiritual self-assurance
of the Puritan elect—"men that think no sin can hurt
them because they are *elect* and that every sin makes
every other man a Reprobate" *(Sermons,* 9:119). He deplores their indifference to the institution and traditions
of the Church. In Puritanism the doctrine which makes
man nothing and God all in the process of salvation ends
in the paradox of spiritual pride and individualism. "The
present Pharisee, the Separatist, that overvalues himself,
and bids us stand farther off . . . separates himself from
our Church, principally for matter of Government and
Discipline, and imagines a Church that shall be defective
in nothing, and does not think himself to be of that
Church, but sometimes to be that Church, for none but
himself is of that persuasion" *(Sermons,* 9:168–69).

Donne is more concerned than Luther or Calvin to
protect himself from the charge of antinomianism. There
is a law, he would have it, which we are meant to follow,
and it is a dangerous error to suppose that we can leave
the whole business of our salvation to God (cf. *Sermons,*

51. *The Sermons of John Donne,* vol. 10, ed. Evelyn M. Simpson
and George R. Potter (Berkeley and Los Angeles, 1962), pp. 346,
296.

7:335–54). Whereas Luther had severed the connection between *fides* and *caritas,* Donne would seem to restore it, at least to the extent of asking us to recognize that virtue is consistent with devotion. The reformers had said as much, but the drift of Puritanism, to a beleaguered representative of the Church of England, seemed to threaten to deny it with a new casuistry of "irresistible grace." The power of sin in us is such, Donne suggests in an early sermon, that grace alone will not wholly make us over to God. "Hath any man felt the grace of God work so upon him at any time, as that he hath concurred fully, intirely with that grace, without any resistance, any slackness?" We must condition ourselves for grace and prepare to receive it, for while Christ promises "to come to the door, and to stand at the door, and to enter if any man open . . . he does not say, he will break open the door: it was not his pleasure to express such an earnestness, such an Irresistibility in his grace so." But it appears to be primarily a controversialist's point, scored against the Puritans' too familiar way with mysteries. "Resistibility, and Irresistibility of grace, which is every Artificers wearing now, was a stuff that our Fathers wore not, a language that pure antiquity spake not. . . . they knew God's pleasure, *Nolumus disputari:* It should scarce be disputed of in the Schools, much less serv'd in every popular pulpit to curious and itching ears; least of all made table-talke, and household-discourse" *(Sermons,* 1:255).[52]

---

52. The *Directions Concerning Preachers* issued by James I in 1628 shows a similar interest in keeping such matters out of the hands of artificers. It forbade all but bishops, or deans "at the least," to preach on "the deep points of predestination, election, reprobation, or of the universality, efficacity, resistibility, or irresistibility of God's grace" *(Documents Illustrative of English Church History,* ed. H. Gee and W. J. Hardy, 4th ed., 1921).

When Donne is not thus fending off the Puritans, his
differences with them on the matter of grace seem slight
enough. Indeed, in the sermon just quoted, while he dis-
allows irresistibility, he allows "infallibility" and seems
to mean nothing different by it: grace can deal defin-
itively with the most resistant will, as in the case of the
thief crucified with Christ, whose conversion illustrates
"the infallibility, and the dispatch of the grace of God
upon them, whom his gracious purpose hath ordained to
salvation: how powerfully he works; how instantly they
obey" *(Sermons,* 1:254). The theme belongs to Donne as
much as to any occupant of a "popular pulpit," and presumably the ears of his audience itched for it as much as
any assembly of Puritans. And certainly his treatment of
it does not consistently give a larger role to human initia-
tive or expand the claim for human merit.

> Without such Grace and such succession of Grace,
> our Will is so far unable to pre-dispose it selfe to
> any good, as that *nec seipso, homo, nisi perniciose
> uti potest* . . . we have no interest in our selves, no
> power to doe anything of, or with our selves, but
> to our destruction. Miserable man! a Toad is a bag
> of Poyson, and a Spider is a blister of Poyson, and
> yet a Toad and a Spider cannot poyson themselves;
> man hath a dram of poyson, originall-Sin in an in-
> visible corner, we know not where, and he cannot
> choose but poyson himself and all his actions with
> that; we are so far from being able to begin without
> Grace, as then when we have the first Grace, we can-
> not proceed to the use of that without more.
> [*Sermons,* 1:293]

He is as precise as Taylor in his use of the nomenclature
of Reformation theology. The grace which provokes the
faith which leads to justification is *preventing* or *pre-*

venient: "no man can prepare that worke, no man can begin it, no man can proceed in it of himselfe. The desire and the actual beginning is from the preventing grace of God" *(Sermons,* 2:305).[53]

This has very much the look of "breaking down the door," an operation of grace which we have seen Donne denying in his strictures on Puritan arrogance and irrationalism. But nothing is more characteristic of Reformation attitudes than the sense of total dependence on God, and nothing derives more naturally from that sense than the notion of sudden conversion, which like other benefits from God may come mysteriously and in forms not immediately suggestive of mercy. Donne's most famous statements on the subject occur in the *Divine Poems:*

> Be this my Text, my Sermon to mine owne
> Therefore that he may raise the Lord throws down.[54]

The sermons, inevitably, develop the same themes, and with the inevitable support of Paul and Augustine. Grace may come as "vehement calamity," but when it does, "yet I can say with his blessed servant Augustine, *Et cum blandiris pater es, & pater es cum caedis,* I feele the hand

53. This conception continues to be part of the popular teaching of Anglicanism at the end of the century and beyond. Cf. Burnet commenting on the tenth of the *Thirty-nine Articles:* "there is a *preventing* Grace, by which the Will is first moved and disposed to turn to God" *(An Exposition of the Thirty-nine Articles of the Church of England* [London, 1699], p. 120).

54. Cf. Samuel Clarke's account of the conversion of the Puritan Robert Bolton, upon whom the Lord acted with a vigor which He usually reserves for "such strong vessels, as he intendeth for strong encounters, and rare employments; for the Lord ranne upon him as a Giant, taking him by the neck, and shaking him to pieces, as he did *Iob;* beating him to the ground as he did Paul, by laying before him the ugly visage of his sins, which lay so heavy upon him that he roared for anguish of heart" *The Marrow of Ecclesiastical History,* 2d ed. [1654], p. 925).

of a father upon me when thou strokest me, and when
thou strikest me I feele the hand of a father too"
(*Sermons*, 8:320).

Donne is, if anything, more open to the idea of sudden
conversion than the Calvinists, whose scheme of "double
predestination" he sees as a restriction on God's free
saving grace. They "will abridge, and contract the large
mercies of God in Christ, and elude, and frustrate, in a
part, the generall promises of God." They are "Men
that are loth, that God should speak so loud, as to say,
He would have all men saved" (*Sermons*, 9:168–69).
There are hints of this limiting impulse in Augustine,
but the Augustine who spoke loudest to Donne was the
author of the *Confessions*,[55] and he, like the St. Paul
exhibited in the Acts of the Apostles is above all a proof
of the swiftness and inexplicability of God's converting
power. Clearly, the idea had immense attractiveness to
Donne. As Mrs. Simpson has said, Paul's conversion
"came to be a subject dear to Donne's heart." And she
notes that when, as Dean, "he adopted the practice of
preaching himself in the cathedral at the Feast of the
Conversion of St. Paul, he did so not only because the
cathedral was dedicated to St. Paul, but also because of
his own preference"—a preference, of course, extended to
Augustine also, with whom, as with Paul, Mrs. Simpson
suggests Donne may have felt a special sympathy (see
Sermons, 1:140). What Donne makes of the conversion
of Paul can be illustrated with the following early example:

> The first thing then is, the powerfulness and dispatch
> of the grace of God in the conversion of them, who
> are ordained to it. . . . In Saint *Paul*, in his conver-

55. Mrs. Simpson notes that "The *Confessions* seem to have been
the work which Donne knew best" (*Sermons*, 10:348).

sion, God wrought upon him all at once, without any discontinuance; He took him at as much disadvantage for grace to work upon as could be; breathing threatenings and slaughters against the disciples, and provided with Commissions for that persecution. But suddainly there came a light, and suddainly a stroke that humbled him, and suddainly a voice, and suddainly a hand that led him to *Damascus*. After God had laid hold upon him, he never gave him over, till he had accomplished his purpose in him. [*Sermons,* 1:255]

The arch-Augustinians of the English Reformation and seventeenth century were, of course, the Puritans, and a complete study of English Augustinianism would require detailed attention to them. Such figures as Thomas Cartwright, John Dod, William Perkins, and other "spiritual preachers" trouble less than their "Arminian" contemporaries to qualify the positions derived from Paul, Augustine, and the Reformers which define the essential faith of the time. As this chapter was begun, however, with the purpose of outlining that faith in general terms —not recording its adjustments and adaptations among the various religious interests—it would seem superfluous to go extensively into its Puritan mutations. In fact, as we have seen to some extent with Donne and Andrewes and Taylor, it is possible to find the fundamental Augustinian doctrines of the Puritans adequately represented in the doctrines of the anti-Puritans.

A brief look at Bunyan will suffice here, to demonstrate (what is perhaps self-evident) that the Puritans yield nothing in Augustinian zeal to their (Protestant) theological opponents. The title *Grace Abounding to the Chief of Sinners* is itself an epitome of Augustinian doctrine, and the experience recorded in the book is faithful to

the Augustinian pattern established in an extensive
Puritan literature of spiritual autobiography—in a word,
conversion.[56] The unregenerate natural man ("rebellious
against God, and careless of mine own salvation," as
Bunyan describes himself) comes to a vivid sense of his
own evil ("conviction of sin") and of God's infinite mercy,
which makes him a gift of "righteousness"—understood
as the condition of being reconciled to God, rather than
an achieved rectitude (a "spiritual experience" rather
than an "ethical condition").[57] The mercy tends to be
certified by the sin, which these narratives sometimes have
a little difficulty in establishing: Bunyan's sin of bell-
ringing is of a piece with the youthful Augustine's stealing of pears, and it has elements in common with Walton's exaggeration of Donne's rakish excesses in order to
give him the character of a "second Augustine." The
larger the sin, the larger the mercy and the more astonish-
ing the visitation of grace: "Sometimes," says Bunyan,
"when, after sin committed, I have looked for sore
chastisement from the hand of God, the very next that
I have had from him hath been the discovery of his
grace."[58] A minor point of interest worth noting in some
of these conversions is the part played in them by books:
Augustine is set on his way by a page turned to at random
in Scripture; Augustine's *Confessions* is decisive for
Petrarch; Bunyan conveniently demonstrates the unity
of Reformation Augustinism by turning at the critical

56. There are useful discussions of this literature in Roger
Sharrock's introduction to his edition of *Grace Abounding to the
Chief of Sinners* (Oxford, 1962), and in G. A. Starr, *Defoe and
Spiritual Autobiography* (Princeton, 1965), pp. 3–50.

57. The terms of the distinction are those of A. S. P. Woodhouse,
"Milton, Puritanism and Liberty," *University of Toronto Quarterly*,
4 (1935): 497.

58. *Grace Abounding*, ed. Sharrock, p. 102.

moment to Luther's *Commentary* on St. Paul's *Epistle to the Galatians,* which spoke to him so intimately, he says, that "I found my condition in his experience, so largely and profoundly handled, as if his Book had been written out of my heart."[59]

As we have seen repeatedly, conversion is the device in Reformation theology for ending the rebellion of the self and bringing man into harmonious relation with God. The relation which naturally obtains between them is disharmony and opposition, owing to the creature's withdrawal from the creator and corruption of the good which inheres in all God's works. An early episode in *Pilgrim's Progress* illustrates this division as vividly as the conversion experience of *Grace Abounding,* and with a symbolism that naïvely parallels Augustine's two cities and Luther's two kingdoms. Christian is stopped on his way to the little wicket-gate by Mr. Worldly Wiseman, who, despite his villain's role in Christian's drama of salvation, is evidently not a representative of mere evil. He is "wise" in an authentic sense of the word: he has a realist's understanding of the limits of human possibility and the savvy to get through the world with a minimum of difficulty to himself or others. He advises "weak men" against "meddling with things too high for them" which can cause them to fall into distractions such as "do not only unman men, . . . but they run them upon desperate ventures to obtain they know not what."[60] The speech is an elaborate web of ironic ambiguities. To be "distracted" in Mr. Worldly Wiseman's sense is to desert the purposes of the world and natural man—that is, to follow the true way of the soul to salvation; "they know not what" implicitly recognizes the necessity of faith not

59. Ibid., p. 41.
60. *Pilgrim's Progress,* ed. Blanton Wharey, rev. Roger Sharrock (Oxford, 1960), p. 18.

to rest within the limits of earthly certainties; the promise
of faith is indeed "too high" for undeserving man and
therefore a miracle for the Christian to rejoice in; and
to be "unmanned" more than hints at spiritual advantage
—the conquest of natural man.[61] Despite this under-
cutting, however, it seems clear that, given the limitations
of his worldly perspective, Mr. Worldly Wiseman gives
a fairly adequate account of himself in matters both intellectual and moral. He would send Christian off, not to
forbidden pleasures, and not back to the City of Destruction, but to the village of Morality and *honest* Mr.
Legality. Christian would there have "honest neighbors,"
and, indeed, we infer from the sparse population of the
village that persons disinclined to moral effort and indifferent to "credit" do not go there.

The village is, in short, a kind of embryonic utopia
got up along lines consistent with the principles of classical ethics (and not impossible to compare with such
"positive" rational utopias as the Sparta of Plutarch's
"Life of Lycurgus"). Bunyan's village aims at "happy"
life ("with much safety, friendship, and content,") on the
basis of social order and private decency—an end and
means sufficiently commonplace in ethical literature. To
be sure, Civility, the "pretty" son of Mr. Legality, is
damned by Evangelist at the end of the episode as a
hypocrite from whom no help can be expected. It is clear,
however, that Bunyan means to suggest more by his name
than deceptive ingratiatingness of manner. He stands also
for the ideals of citizenship and the goals of social col-
lectivity—suggested again in the same sentence which
introduces Civility by the reference to "honest neighbors"
and the mention of Christian's wife and children, who

61. Cf. Bishop Burnet: "somewhat of the Man enters into all that
men do: We are made up of infirmities" (*An Exposition of the
Thirty-nine Articles,* p. 129).

can join him, says Mr. Worldly Wiseman, if he will give up his journeying and settle in the village of Morality. Finally, it puts no strain on Bunyan's text, I believe, to find in the mention of the "reasonable rates" of living in the village a slur on the life of reason, so disastrously inferior to the life of faith.

The episode is a considerable problem unless understood in terms of Reformation dualism. Why, after all, is it not good to be as good as we can? The life of reason and moral effort which aims at earthly happiness *is* of course good, as long as one considers it within the limited context of practical affairs—the government of nations and families and the ordering of the individual existence. Legality and Civility well serve the honest neighbors who dwell in Morality with safety, friendship, and content. But Christian approaches the village only to find his burden of sin growing heavier and to be threatened with destruction by having the hill fall on his head. In starting for Morality he has strayed from the way of grace, Evangelist tells him, "almost to the hazardship of thy perdition."

Evangelist is an appropriate figure with whom to end this survey, for he concentrates the vision that unites Paul, Augustine, Luther, Calvin, the English Reformers and semi-Arminians, the Presbyterians, and sectaries with a simplicity and force that obliterates their differences. He sees exclusively what they see principally: man's sinfulness and need of salvation, the revelation of God's grace in Christ, the necessity of faith—and the blind and vicious irrelevance of every motion of the human spirit not focused on these truths. Thus, insofar as the village of Morality represents a merely humanist ideal of the rational ethical life it symbolizes the assertion of human sufficiency in independence of the divine—the perversion of the will that Paul associated with the flesh, which

Augustine called "concupiscence," and which defines the spirit of the earthly city in its better as well as worse aspects. Insofar as the village represents the ambition of human effort in salvation (Mr. Worldly Wiseman goes there *to church*), it symbolizes the still greater error of confusing the claims of the earthly and heavenly cities, the blasphemous and prideful denial of the sovereignty of God and the refusal of his love on the only terms he chooses to give it. Legality and Civility can survive there, but to Christian it means death.

3 Meditation

The Augustinian and Protestant theological background that I have been claiming to be relevant to seventeenth-century English religious poetry is, of course, not the only background that might be suggested, and it appears, indeed, to conflict with the most comprehensive account that has been given of the informing sources of metaphysical poetry—Louis L. Martz's study of poetry's debt to meditation, the systematically formulated practices of Catholic devotion, given their most influential form in St. Ignatius's *Spiritual Exercises* (1548).[1] On the face of it, it appears unlikely that Jesuit and Protestant traditions could equally sustain the metaphysicals, or could encourage similar qualities in poetry. Indeed, Ignatius's *Spiritual Exercises* has seemed to epitomize the Catholic alternative to Protestant theologies of grace. A recent history of the Reformation puts the contrast clearly:

> Luther came out of his spiritual struggle convinced that man's sinfulness is inherent, that he cannot save

1. *The Poetry of Meditation: A Study in English Religious Literature of the Seventeenth Century*, 2d ed. (New Haven, 1962).

himself and that only a merciful God can save him.
Loyola came out of his struggle believing that both
God and Satan are external to man, that man has
the power to choose between them, and that by the
disciplined use of his imagination—vividly picturing
to himself, for instance, the horrors of hell and the
sufferings of Christ—he can so strengthen his will as
to make the choice for God. Where Luther and Protestantism ended in a belief in predestination and the
utter sovereignty of God, Loyola and the Catholic
Church insisted upon man's free will and his power
to cooperate with God—even, according to Loyola,
to the point of influencing the course of the battle
between the armies of God and of Satan by his choice.
Luther denied man's free will; Loyola glorified it and
set out to discipline it by the use of imagination. The
record of his method [is] *Spiritual Exercises*.[2]

Clearly, Luther had a much stronger position in Protestant England than Loyola. Martz has no difficulty in showing, however, that the Ignatian method of meditation,
though bearing very obviously the impress of continental
Catholicism, was widely available to seventeenth-century
Englishmen and widely welcome among them. Presses were
busy printing Catholic books in English at Antwerp, Lou-
vain, Rouen, Paris, Douay, Rheims, and secretly, in England itself. Official vigilance did not prevent wholesale
importation and distribution of these books, sizable num-
bers of which were manuals of meditation. Martz describes
a "flood" of such treatises which "poured into England"
during the first half of the seventeenth century. There is
plentiful bibliographic as well as poetic evidence then to
support the view that "a large proportion of the English

2. E. Harris Harbison, *The Age of Reformation* (Ithaca, N.Y.,
1955), pp. 83–84.

public had taken to its heart the fruits of the Counter-Reformation in the realm of inward devotion."[3]

No such hospitableness appeared in the English response to Catholic theology, to the Church as an institution, or to that spearhead of the Counter-Reformation abroad, the Society of Jesus. Catholic devotional writing and practices were Rome's almost uniquely acceptable offering to Protestant England.[4] The reasons for their acceptability seem sufficiently clear: the Reformation had itself been a revolution conducted in the name of devotional religion, and it had insisted—against Roman formalism and sacramentalism—on the internalizing of the spiritual life. Protestantism had not, however, developed a separate devotional literature—in part, perhaps, because its theology itself sounded devotional themes so strongly, but also because the work of establishing the dogmatic essentials of Reformation doctrine had occupied it fully. "The Reformation of religion in the western churches," wrote Jeremy Taylor, "hath been so universally opposed by evil spirits and evil men . . . that it was found to be work enough for the ministers of religion to convince the gainsayers." In such circumstances some obviously important matters had to be left "loosely, till they could discern whether the house would be burnt or no by the great flames which then brake out." The resulting lacks had needed to be supplied, and, as Taylor said of another of them, "we were forced to go down to the forges of the Philistines . . . for we were almost wholly unprovided."[5]

In the matter of doctrine there is no question but that

3. *Poetry of Meditation*, pp. 7, 9.

4. Roman moral theology and casuistry became a second acceptable offering to the Caroline divines. See H. R. McAdoo, *The Structure of Caroline Moral Theology* (London, 1949).

5. Jeremy Taylor, *The Whole Works*, ed. Heber and Eden (London, 1883), 9.vi.

English seventeenth-century poets went only to Reformation forges. (One makes the necessary exception in the case of Crashaw.) Thus, for example, the Holy Sonnets, which in method provide "strong evidence for the profound impact of early Jesuit training upon the later career of John Donne,"[6] on every point of doctrine provide strong evidence of Protestantism. The poet who prays "impute me righteous" is imagining the process of salvation in explicitly Protestant terms. The imputation of righteousness is God's act of forgiveness, a quite different operation of grace from that imagined in most Catholic theology, which has generally considered righteousness (as in Aquinas and in the Trentine formulations) to be a created quality—which the human will cooperates in bringing about—giving man the merit which he lacks in his unjustified state (a righteousness "imparted" rather than "imputed"). Whatever Donne's perplexities in his early *Satyre: Of Religion,* there is no appearance in the doctrine of the Holy Sonnets either of the crypto-Catholic or of one who "in strange way . . . stands inquiring right." The later poems demonstrate a precise understanding of the issues in the debate over the nature of grace and come out unequivocally on the Protestant side. The Reformation sponsors of the doctrine of "preventing" or "prevenient" grace—the grace which is required to make men *want* to be saved by softening the stony in their hearts—would acknowledge their share in the question and Donne's implicit answer in the lines "Yet grace, if thou repent, thou canst not lacke; / But who shall give thee that grace to beginne?" *(Holy Sonnet* 2).[7]

Martz's argument for the influence of Catholic meditation on English poetry does not turn on parallels of doc-

6. Martz, *Poetry of Meditation,* p. 53.
7. In all references to the Holy Sonnets I have used the numbering of Helen Gardner's edition, *Divine Poems* (Oxford, 1952).

trine, however, but on parallels of form—a peculiar three-part organization—and of imaginative strategy: the application of the senses to make vivid the subjects of pious reflection, introspective analysis, and dramatization. His evidence deserves minute attention in any attempt to illuminate a relation between the ideas of the period and its literature, and can help confirm the suggestion of the present study that there is a quite direct relation between the structure of the religious imagination in the seventeenth century and the structure of poems. Despite the un-Augustinian and un-Protestant value which Loyola's system of meditation places on reason and will, it duplicates the Protestant emphasis on individual religious experience, is burdened with a Protestant-like sense of the distance that separates God from man and of the catastrophic deficiencies of man responsible for the separation, and dramatizes the possibility of a sudden healing of the breach. It provides then another vehicle for the imagination of dualism, miraculism, and conversion which is characteristic of the period of the Augustinian revival and which, I have been maintaining, constitutes the essential background of ideas for a body of religious poetry designed to act out reconciliations. One gets glimpses of these reconciling possibilities in the definition of meditation which Martz quotes from St. Francis of Sales and which he cites as the central definition for his own study.

Every meditation is a thought, but every thought is not a meditation. . . . but when we thinke of heavenly things, not to learne but to love them, that is called to meditate: and the exercise thereof Meditation: in which our mynd, not as a flie, by simple musing, nor yet as a locust, to eate and be filled, but as a sacred Bee flies amongst the flowres of holy mysteries, to extract from them the honie of Divine Love. In fine, thoughtes and studies may be upon any subject, but meditation in our present sense, hath reference onely to those obiects, whose consideration tend's to make us good and devote. So that Meditation is an attentive thought iterated, or voluntarily intertained in the mynd, to excitate the will to holy affections and res-olutions.[8]

The Spiritual Exercises of St. Ignatius, the freely used basis of the systems of meditation developed in the century to follow, was designed to provide the structure for a month's devotions, taking the exercitant through precisely distinguished stages. The course is charted in a paragraph of Ignatius's Introductory Observations: "Four Weeks are assigned to the Exercises. . . . This corresponds to the four parts into which they are divided, namely: The first part, which is devoted to the consideration and contem-plation of sin; the second part, which is taken up with the life of Christ our Lord up to Palm Sunday inclusive; the third part, which treats of the passion of Christ our Lord; the fourth part, which deals with the Resurrection and Ascension."[9]

A single exercise—repeated several times during the day in which it was assigned—is essentially a three-part structure utilizing methodically the three "powers of the soul": memory, understanding, and will. The first part, consisting of two "preludes," follows an introduc-tory prayer. The first prelude is the "composition of place," which Martz suggests taught metaphysical poets lessons in concreteness and dramatic immediacy. It is an effort to see in the imagination things not visible to the eye, as in a meditation on sin to "see in imagination my

8. *Poetry of Meditation*, pp. 14–15.
9. See *The Spiritual Exercises of St. Ignatius*, trans. Louis J. Puhl, S.J. (Westminster, Md., 1959).

soul as a prisoner in this corruptible body, and to consider my whole composite being as an exile here on
earth, cast out to live among brute beasts." The second
prelude asks for an appropriate emotion. It anticipates
("premeditates") the spiritual condition, or mood, to be
achieved in the meditation which follows (the "points"
and "colloquy") and makes plain the direct affective intention of the "art of meditation." Thus the second prelude of a meditation on sin might "ask for shame and
confusion, because I see how many have been lost on
account of a single mortal sin, and how many times I
have deserved eternal damnation, because of the many
grievous sins that I have committed."[10]

It will be useful for the purposes of this study, which
are not identical with Martz's, to reprint the instructions
for the remaining parts of a complete exercise. The
rhythm of the whole will show its "reconciling" impetus.

> Second Exercise [of the first week]
> *This is a meditation on our sins. After the prepa-
> ratory prayer and two preludes there are five points
> and a colloquy.*
> *Prayer.* The preparatory prayer will be the same
> [through all four weeks. It begs for "grace that all
> my intentions, actions, and operations may be di-
> rected purely to the praise and service of his Divine
> Majesty."]
> *First Point* (following Preludes). This is the record
> of my sins. I will call to mind all the sins of my life,
> reviewing year by year and period by period. Three
> things will help me in this: First to consider the place
> where I lived; secondly, my dealings with others;
> thirdly, the office I have held.
> *Second Point.* I will weigh the gravity of my sins,

10. *Spiritual Exercises,* pp. 25–26.

and see the loathesomeness and malice which every mortal sin I have committed has in itself, even though it were not forbidden.

Third Point. I will consider who I am, and by means of examples, humble myself:

1. What am I compared with all men?
2. What are all men compared with the angels and saints of paradise?
3. Consider what all creation is in comparison with God. Then I alone, what can I be?
4. I will consider all the corruption and loathesomeness of my body.
5. I will consider myself as a source of corruption and contagion from which has issued countless sins and evils and the most offensive poison.

Fourth Point. I will consider who God is against whom I have sinned, going through His attributes and comparing them with their contraries in me: His wisdom with my ignorance, His power with my weakness, His justice with my iniquity, His goodness with my wickedness.

Fifth Point. This is a cry of wonder accompanied by surging emotion as I pass in review all creatures. How is it that they have permitted me to live and sustained me in life! Why have the angels, though they are the sword of God's justice, tolerated me, guarded me, and prayed for me! Why have the saints interceded for me and asked favors for me! And the heavens, sun, moon, stars, and the elements; the fruits, birds, fishes and other animals—why have they all been at my service! How is it that the earth did not open to swallow me up, and create new hells in which I shall be tormented forever!

Colloquy. I will conclude with a colloquy, extolling the mercy of God our Lord, pouring out my

> thoughts to Him, and giving thanks to Him that up
> to this very moment he has granted me life. I will
> resolve with His grace to amend for the future.
> Close with an *Our Father*.[11]

What is perhaps most immediately striking in this is
the systematic stirring up of intense feeling.[12] Helen
Gardner, in commenting on Donne's Holy Sonnets, has
mentioned "the meditation's deliberate stimulation of
emotion," and it deserves note that in the Ignatian system
this deliberate stimulation is made explicitly the function of understanding and will. "The understanding is
used to think over the matter more in detail, and then
the will to rouse more deeply the emotions,"[13] until, by
systematic concentration, it can produce "a cry of wonder
accompanied by surging emotion" (Fifth Point above).
The metaphysicals' celebrated "blend of passion and
thought" is, presumably, anticipated in this process in
which the mind simply thinks itself into passion.

More to our purpose, however, is that in its total
movement, the meditation on sin, like the whole four
weeks, proceeds through self-induced despairs and dev-
astations to a mood in which it is possible to talk with
God (colloquy) and be assured of his mercy. Thus meditation would seem likely to lend itself in poetry not only
to exaggerated emotional intensities, but also to such
emphatic reconciliations as we have seen occurring—and

11. *Spiritual Exercises*, pp. 29–30.
12. The exciting of intense and appropriate emotion is a chief
end of the meditative process. Thus, for example, the exercitant
should make a general confession during the time of the Exercises,
according to Ignatius, as there will then "be much greater merit
and profit, because of the greater sorrow experienced for all the
sins and perversities of his whole life." Intensities of sorrow then
lead to intensities of joy, hope, and love.
13. *Spiritual Exercises*, p. 27.

in fact occurring in colloquy—in "Goodfriday, 1613.
Riding Westward." The pattern is clearly suggested again
in the Holy Sonnets. Holy Sonnet 2, for example, while
not developing into a colloquy in which God is addressed
(instead the soul is addressed throughout), moves surely
from the soul's sin to Christ's redemptive power.

> Oh my blacke Soule! now thou art summoned
> By sicknesse, deaths herald, and champion;
> Thou art like a pilgrim, which abroad hath done
> Treason, and durst not turne to whence hee is fled,
> Or like a thiefe, which till deaths doome be read,
> Wisheth himselfe delivered from prison;
> But damn'd and hal'd to execution,
> Wisheth that still he might be imprisoned;
> Yet grace, if thou repent, thou canst not lacke;
> But who shall give thee that grace to beginne?
> Oh make thy selfe with holy mourning blacke,
> And red with blushing, as thou art with sinne;
> Or wash thee in Christs blood, which hath this might
> That being red, it dyes red soules to white.

Reconciliation is given a larger place in some of these
poems, as when Donne treats colloquy in the style envisaged in Luis de La Puente's *Meditations:* "as the bride
speaketh to her spouse."[14] This is the style, for example,
of Sonnet 10—"Batter my heart, three person'd God,"
which is a kind of colloquy throughout, coming to a
climactic, sexually explicit conclusion:

> Take mee to you, imprison mee, for I
> Except you'enthrall mee, never shall be free,
> Nor ever chast, except you ravish mee.

But in all, the rising rhythm, the ascent to reconciliation,
is unmistakable, and such a development is, as we have

14. Quoted in Martz, *Poetry of Meditation,* p. 37.

seen, consistent with the rhythm of meditation. Ignatius looks for "desolation" and "consolation" as the "spiritual experiences" which meditation should produce,[15] and arranges for the second infallibly to follow the first, not only in the meditation on sin, but in the larger pattern of the whole four weeks. He distinguishes between the "purgative" first week and its "illuminative" successors,[16] each more intent upon what St. Francis of Sales called "the honie of Divine Love." "The ultimate goal," as Martz has said, is "to move from Fear to Charity, from distrust of the self to confidence in God."[17] Such a reconciling movement manifests itself strongly again in Helen Gardner's restoration of the order of the twelve Holy Sonnets which were printed in the 1633 edition of Donne's *Divine Poems*.[18] They fall into two groups of six, the first (desolating) occupied with death and the evil of the human soul, the second (consoling) occupied with God's love of man as made manifest in man's favoured place in the animal creation and in God's willingness to redeem man from sin. The distance between the two groups, and the direction of meditation, can be judged by comparing "Oh my blacke Soule" above, the second in the sequence, with the eleventh.

Wilt thou love God, as he thee! then digest,
My Soule, this wholsome meditation,
How God the Spirit, by Angels waited on
In heaven, doth make his Temple in thy brest,
The Father having begot a Sonne most blest,

15. *Spiritual Exercises*, p. 3.
16. *Spiritual Exercises*, p. 4.
17. *Poetry of Meditation*, p. 150.
18. The restoration makes a coherent sequence of the sonnets numbered 2, 4, 6, 7, 9, 10, 11, 12, 13, 14, 15, 16 in Grierson's edition and fully justifies Miss Gardner's revival of their manuscript designation as "Divine Meditations."

And still begetting, (for he ne'r begonne)
Hath deign'd to chuse thee by adoption,
Coheire to'his glory, and Sabbaths endlesse rest;
And as a robb'd man, which by search doth finde
His stolne stuffe sold, must lose or buy'it againe:
The Sonne of Glory came downe, and was slaine,
Us whom he'had made, and Satan stolne, to unbinde.
'Twas much, that man was made like God before,
But, that God should be made like man, much more.

This discussion of the Holy Sonnets would suggest
that they were written according to a formula that could
produce only "poetry of exclusion"—to recur again to
Richards's term for poetry which commits itself to the
suppression of emotional ambiguities. I have stressed the
methodical cultivation of single states of emotion that is
encouraged in meditation: the straightforward utterance,
the careful deliberation that imagines each step before
it is taken and plots out a complete emotional development so as to leave nothing to chance and admit nothing
not relevant to the single emotional effect that is desired.
Thus the first sonnet of the series indicates the complete
range of possibilities to be allowed, establishing the limits
of subject matter and emotion and locating the highs
and lows. Its function in the series, Helen Gardner remarks, is analogous to that of the preparatory prayer in
meditation. "Donne begins his set of sonnets on the Last
Things," says Miss Gardner, "in the proper manner with a
preparatory prayer. In the octave of the first sonnet he re-
collects himself, remembers his creation and redemption
and that he has received the gift of the Holy Spirit; in
the sestet he laments the power of the devil upon him
and asks for grace.")[19]
This rigor of "exclusiveness" is not incompatible with

19. *Divine Poems* p. li.

certain qualities associated with a dialectical method. Plainly, it is not the poetic situation insisted upon by Murray Krieger, in which the poet is required not to "stack the cards"[20] but to reflect the contradictions and oppositions of experience as honestly and directly as does—I suggest the implicit analogue—the realistic novelist, whose honesty in this regard is perhaps only a function of his being theologically uncommitted and incurious. Rather, the poetry of meditation is minutely stacked, with a view to producing what is in the language of poetics a "resolution" (or "reconciliation") and in the language of religion a "consolation" (or "reconciliation").

Reconciliation and consolation are points of rest, however, which require as a precondition unrest, or at least, as we saw in "Riding Westward," the appearance of unrest. There must be at least an ostensible clash of apparent incompatibles. "Dialectic" in the Holy Sonnets obviously goes this far and no farther. Within a secure framework of belief which affirms at the outset (as in the sonnet of "preparatory prayer") that man is God's creature designed to serve God's ends ("made by thee and for thee") and redeemed by Christ's sacrifice, they attempt to give scope to the exertions of the soul in its independent motion. It is not a wide scope, to be sure, but the attempt is evident to make contrasts sharp and oppositions absolute: the soul, black with its own sin and driven by its own urgencies to destruction, is washed white by Christ's sacrifice. The will, reformed in meditation, is shown reforming in the Holy Sonnets—overcoming its impulses to waywardness, its involvement with "the world, the flesh, and devill," requesting to be made acceptable to God ("imputed righteous") and learning the

20. *The Tragic Vision* (New York, 1960), pp. 241–42.

lessons of love. That the lessons shall be learned, which is necessitated by the explicit plan of such a sequence, means, of course, that resolution is achieved by a device of manipulation or suppression: the will, in its restricted human function, is constructed to collapse. It is essential to the dialectic and dramatic character of these poems, however, that it be allowed to make at least a momentary stand: dramatized reconciliation can come only out of dramatized opposition.

But, as we have seen, it is not only the strategies of opposition and reconciliation that seem to tie the "meditative poem" as exemplified by the Holy Sonnets to the Augustinian tradition; it is equally the nature of the forces opposed and reconciled. Such poems focus powerfully on the contrast between man's refractoriness and the duty owed to God, between man's sterile self-attention and God's encompassing love. They are "metaphysical" in an exact sense in centering on a conflict between conceptions of the "real": on the one side, meaning and existence as defined by the limited human mind and in the context of practical (or perverse) human purposes; on the other, meaning and existence as defined by God and the religiously instructed human soul. English poets of the seventeenth century, inescapably Augustinian and Protestant, with their metaphysical sensitivities supported, as the evidence of Martz and Gardner suggests, by the literature and the practice of meditation, are above all preoccupied with this conflict and with the necessity of stacking the cards in favor of religious definitions against the merely human.

It is clear, of course, that the metaphysicals are not simply the poetical step-children of Loyola, but participate with him in a very general movement of religious revival and reaction which challenges the humanist positions of the earlier Renaissance. Several studies have dis-

cussed this movement as a "Counter-Renaissance"; others
have expanded the term "Mannerist" from its purely art
historical uses to include antihumanist, anticlassical developments pervasive in European culture after the
decades of the High Renaissance.[21] An aspect of this
movement which was briefly discussed in an earlier
chapter was its specific hostility to the rationalist ethics
of Aristotle, which considered man's "function" to be
rational activity and his "end" to be earthly happiness
(a condition essentially dependent on reason and virtue,
but assisted by such external aids as riches, health, and
honor). There is interest, therefore, in Loyola's opposing
conception of human functions and ends in the section
of his work which explains the "First Principle and
Foundation of Meditation."

> Man is created to praise, reverence, and serve God
> our Lord, and by this means to save his soul.

> The other things in the face of the earth are created
> for man to help him in attaining the end for which
> he is created.

> Hence, man is to make use of them in as far as they
> help him in the attainment of his end, and he must
> rid himself of them in as far as they prove a hin-
> drance to him.

> Therefore, we must make ourselves indifferent to all
> created things, as far as we are allowed free choice
> and are not under any prohibition. Consequently, as
> far as we are concerned, we should not prefer health
> to sickness, riches to poverty, honor to dishonor, a

21. Most importantly Arnold Hauser's *Mannerism: The Crisis
of the Renaissance and the Origin of Modern Art* (New York,
1965).

long life to a short life. The same holds for all other things.

Our one desire and choice should be what is more conducive to the end for which we are created.[22]

But Loyola's intention to turn Aristotle upside-down is, of course, simply incidental to the spirit which makes him congenial to the metaphysicals. For, despite a certain chariness of the subject of grace (the seventeenth of his "Rules for Thinking with the Church" warns against too much speaking of it lest the heresy be encouraged "whereby liberty [free will] be taken away") his method is dominated by that idea, and he is as close to the English metaphysicals in theological disposition as he is distant in dogma. Grace and conversion are the "longer flight" anticipated and imagined in *Spiritual Exercises*—which is itself, as a Protestant writer has said, "the rescript of St. Ignatius' own experience of conversion."[23] Certainly such an experience would seem to be being drawn on when, in the Week primarily devoted to "Election," Ignatius describes the soul's response "when our Lord God so moves and attracts the will that without doubt or power of doubting, the devout soul follows what is shown her." In imagining the passivity of the soul in this process, Ignatius is closer to Luther than Aquinas, as others—including Benedictine objectors—have noticed, and he announces a temper in Catholic piety that suggests alignment with the reconciling urgencies of the Protestant Reformation. Conversion appears to have been the decisive fact for him as for the age, and it perhaps

22. *Spiritual Exercises,* p. 12.
23. Frank Gavin, "The Medieval and Modern Roman Conceptions of Grace," *The Doctrine of Grace,* ed. W. T. Whitely (London, 1932), p. 162.

explains more than has been suspected about the age, and its literature, that

> Reformation and Counter-Reformation alike were the achievements of "twice-born men" . . . souls who experienced [or who lived in the desire and expectation of experiencing] the Grace of God in individual lives. At once removed and detached, poles apart from his Protestant contemporaries, the Founder of the Jesuits is yet at one with them in the sharing of a transforming and catastrophic experience of grace,—immediate, direct and personal."[24]

24. Ibid.

4 Herbert

In treating George Herbert as a poet in whom Reformation ideas play an important and informing role, one confronts a rival thesis powerfully supported. Rosamund Tuve was a gifted reader of Herbert who understood intimately the way his mind worked in poetry.[1] It was one of her special missions returned to in several books, however, to correct what she saw as the modern error of treating the periods of literary history as a succession of discontinuous self-sufficient units, and she devoted great learning and energy to proving the continuity of the Renaissance with the seventeenth century and the seminal importance of the Middle Ages to both. The cause was a good one, but one of its casualties was the Reformation, which tended

1. Rosamund Tuve, *A Reading of George Herbert* (Chicago, 1952). Joseph H. Summers's important book, *George Herbert: His Religion and Art* (Cambridge, Mass., 1954), gives the Reformation greater prominence among the influences which shaped Herbert's religious-philosophical position. He seems to me less exact than Miss Tuve, however (who neglects it entirely), in defining the quality of religious experience and emotion in the poems.

to become invisible in her long view of antecedent Christianity. Luther and Calvin had little to say to her that could not be found in medieval Augustinians, and she was indifferent to the scale and suddenness of the Augustinian efflorescence that occurred in the sixteenth century and dominated the mental life of the seventeenth. Characteristically, in her last book *(Allegorical Imagery,* 1965) she argues for an essentially Augustinian understanding (though not so named) of the "gift virtues" personified in *The Faerie Queene* while, at the same time, rejoicing in the "recapture of Spenser from the ranks of the Calvinists."

I do not intend to claim Herbert for the Calvinists, but I shall try to insist on the essentially Protestant and Augustinian nature of his preoccupations and to show that in him, as in other seventeenth-century poets, these preoccupations tend naturally to achieve expression in forms characteristic of what I have been calling the poetry of reconciliation. One can scarcely avoid citing as a leading example "The Collar," Herbert's most famous and most becommented poem.

> I Struck the board, and cry'd, No more.
> I will abroad.
> What? shall I ever sigh and pine?
> My lines and life are free; free as the rode,
> Loose as the winde, as large as store.
> Shall I be still in suit?
> Have I no harvest but a thorn
> To let me bloud, and not restore
> What I have lost with cordiall fruit?
> Sure there was wine
> Before my sighs did drie it: there was corn
> Before my tears did drown it.
> Is the yeare onely lost to me?

Have I no bayes to crown it?
No flowers, no garlands gay? all blasted?
All wasted?
Not so, my heart: but there is fruit,
And thou hast hands.
Recover all thy sigh-blown age
On double pleasures: leave thy cold dispute
Of what is fit, and not. Forsake thy cage,
Thy rope of sands,
Which pettie thoughts have made, and made to thee
Good cable, to enforce and draw,
And be thy law,
While thou didst wink and wouldst not see.
Away; take heed:
I will abroad.
Call in thy deaths head there: tie up thy fears.
He that forbears
To suit and serve his need,
Deserves his load.
But as I rav'd and grew more fierce and wilde
At every word,
Me thoughts I heard one calling, *Child!*
And I reply'd, *My Lord.*[2]

The poem is a virtuoso dramatization of that warfare of the will which engaged the Augustinian imagination. Mere human energy of self-assertion—"concupiscence," in Augustine's word, or pride—assails the constraints put upon it by the necessity to bend to God's command. In its blind recalcitrance, the human will sees nothing of God except the aspect of constraint and command and fails to grasp the relation between these and God's love.

2. *The Works of George Herbert*, ed. F. E. Hutchinson (Oxford, 1941), p. 153. All subsequent citations are to this edition.

In resisting God's will it rejects its own good, as, in refus-
ing to make the small renunciations called for by the
divine discipline, it refuses its immense rewards. Self-
regard and regard for the goods of the world are a denial
of the self's real interests, as the poem underlines with
insistent irony: the "bayes" that crown earthly glory are
nothing beside the glory promised by the crown of thorns;
the "freedom" to go abroad (i.e. to follow the self's own
impulses away from God) is nothing beside the freedom
to obey; the "cordiall fruit" which the world provides
falls disastrously short of God's love in restorative power;
the corn and wine enjoyed by those who thrive in the
world cannot be considered goods in any sense, when
perversely preferred to the bread and wine of the sacra-
ment.

One of Herbert's differences as a man of the Reformation from his more extreme Calvinistic countrymen is
clear in the last comparison: for him the euchaï ist is holy
and an essential part of Christian worship.[3] It will help to
clarify his position vis-à-vis Reformation Augustinianism,
however, to compare "The Collar" as a statement concerning the rewards of the Christian (and, possibly, of
the Christian clergyman) with a statement on the same
subject from Calvin's explication of John 4: 36–38:

> And he who reapeth receiveth reward, and gathereth
> fruit into life eternal; that both he that soweth, and
> he that reapeth, may rejoice together. For in this is
> the saying true, That there is one who soweth, and
> another who reapeth. I sent you to reap that on
> which you did not labour; other men laboured, and
> you have entered into their labours.

3. But see Malcolm Ross, *Poetry and Dogma* (New Brunswick,
N.J., 1954), on decay of Eucharistic symbolism in metaphysical poets.

Calvin comments as follows:

> *And he who reapeth receiveth reward.* How dili-
> gently we ought to devote ourselves to the work of
> God . . . because a large and most excellent reward
> is reserved for our labour; for [Jesus] promises that
> there will be *fruit,* and *fruit* not corruptible or fad-
> ing. What he adds about *fruit* may be explained in
> two ways; either it is an announcement of the *re-
> ward,* and on that supposition he would say the same
> thing twice in different words; or, he applauds the
> labours of those who enrich the kingdom of God, as
> we shall afterwards find him repeating, *I have chosen
> you, that you may go and bear fruit, and that your
> fruit may remain,* (John xv. 16.) And certainly both
> considerations ought greatly to encourage the min-
> isters of the word, that they may never sink under
> the toil, when they hear that a crown of glory is
> prepared for them in heaven, and know that the
> *fruit* of their *harvest* will not only be precious in the
> sight of God, but will also be eternal. It is for this
> purpose of leading us to judge from it as to the merits
> of works; for which of us, if we come to a reckoning,
> will not be found more worthy of being punished
> for slothfulness than of being *rewarded* for diligence.
> To the best labourers nothing else will be left than
> to approach to God in all humility to implore for-
> giveness. But the Lord, who acts toward us with the
> kindness of a father, in order to correct our sloth,
> and to encourage us who would otherwise be dis-
> mayed, deigns to bestow upon us an undeserved
> reward.
>   This is so far from overturning justification by
> faith that it rather confirms it. For, in the first place,
> how comes it that God finds in us any thing to *re-*

ward, but because He has bestowed it upon us by
his Spirit? Now we know that the Spirit is the earnest
and pledge of adoption, (Eph. i. 14.) Secondly, how
comes it that God confers so great honour on im-
perfect and sinful works but because, after having
by free grace reconciled us to himself, He accepts
our works without any regard to merit, by not im-
puting the sins which cleave to them?[4]

One finds interest in the repeated, if traditional, language in Herbert and Calvin of labor, fruit, harvest,
crown, etc.[5] The more significant parallel between "The
Collar" and the passage from Calvin's *Commentary,* however, lies in the conception which they evidently share of
God's characteristic demeanor toward man, man's characteristic demeanor toward God, and the nature of Christian duty. Herbert's poem, up to the last lines, is an argument for the life of man against God. The position is
stated energetically and compellingly, but it is, of course,
wrong, and is wholly overthrown in the last lines with
the remarkable appearance of God the reconciler. Man
should live for God and against himself, a life of entire
self-abnegation, as the New Testament insists. Jesus in
himself symbolized the condition of righteousness as a
slavery to God in which the Christian's whole endeavor is

4. John Calvin, *Commentary on the Gospel According to John,*
trans. William Pringle (Edinburgh, 1847) pp. 171–72.

5. Perhaps the likeliest scriptural source for Herbert's corn and
wine is Psalm 4: 6–7. "There be many that say, Who will shew us
any good? Lord, lift thou up the light of thy countenance upon us.
Thou hast put gladness in my heart, more than in the time that
their corn and their wine increased." This psalm figures in Augustine's account of his conversion, and leads him to reflections resem-
bling Herbert's: "I had in thy eternal Simple Essence other *corn,
and wine, and oil"* (*Confessions,* trans. E. B. Pusey, Everyman's
Library [London, n.d.] pp. 182–83).

to suppress the impulses of the self and to act according to no other will than God's. The purpose of Jesus' own life, in this perspective, "was to work out in a single human life complete obedience to the will of God—to the uttermost, that is, to death."[6] "I can of mine own self do nothing . . . I seek not mine own will, But the will of the Father which hath sent me" (John 5: 30).

But that men are sluggish followers of Christ's example and that God extends himself in love to cover human dereliction is the essence of the Augustinian position. Calvin's theology defines the situation that Herbert has depicted: man essentially wilful and wayward, devoted to his own ends which he blindly misconceives; God desiring only obedience and man self-compelled to disobey; God "Who acts towards us with the kindness of a father," encouraging the human effort of obedience, accepting the inadequate "labour" with love and rewarding it with a "reconciliation" which man is powerless to deserve and to which, Calvin makes clear, human resources and human effort are finally irrelevant, for "how comes it that God finds in us anything to reward, but because he bestowed it upon us by his Spirit?" Herbert describes God's free bestowal of grace in similar terms in the prayer at the end of *The Country Parson* which might be cited as a gloss on many poems in *The Temple* but fits "The Collar" with special closeness:

> But thou Lord, art patience, and pity and sweetnesse, and love; therefore we sons of men are not consumed. Thou hast exalted thy mercy above all things; and hast made our salvation, not our punishment, thy glory: so that then where sin abounded, not death, but grace superabounded; accordingly,

6. Sir Edwin Hoskyns and Noel Davey, *The Riddle of the New Testament* (London, 1958), p. 173.

when we had sinned beyond any help in heaven or earth, then thou saidst, Lo, I come. [*Works,* p. 288]

One of Miss Tuve's purposes in treating Herbert against the background of a tradition "inherited through at least the ten or twelve preceding centuries" is to diminish the element of shock and surprise in the poems, which she considers to have been exaggerated by modern critics whose delight in "metaphysical wit" is rooted in ignorance of the medieval "reading of life." She is properly severe in dealing with certain critical extravagances and does very valuable service in explicating Herbert's iconography, employing methods learned from art history to illuminate obscurities in the imagery and improve the modern reader's sense of what particular kinds of references meant to Herbert and his contemporaries and predecessors. Certainly, we can share her impatience with approaches to Herbert's poetry which aim chiefly at celebrating the "modernities of temper it exhibits." It should be clear, nonetheless, that a poem like "The Collar," for all the traditional quality of its metaphors, has elements of shock and surprise built into it and that, if we resist them, we are resisting a good deal of what Herbert has to say to us and neglecting important features of his art.[7]

7. Summers also tends to lower the temperature of Herbert's poetry, reading it perhaps too exclusively as expressing the mind of the Country Parson. "The command of love to God and one's neighbor meant that each action must be decent, orderly, and edifying as well as charitable. It was impossible to distinguish the aims of specific actions, for all was done to the glory of God: the aid both spiritual and physical of one's neighbor was also an act of worship and the productive life; and any individual act of public or private worship, once communicated, could become an act of edification to one's neighbor. The ultimate method of reflecting God's glory was the creation of a work of decency and order, a work of beauty, whether a church, an ordered poem, or an ordered life" *(George Herbert,* pp. 83–84).

By appealing to a Reformation reading of life instead of the medieval one that Miss Tuve suggests (though not denying continuities), we secure the double benefit of restoring to Herbert an appropriate intellectual background (a guard against random modernizations) and preserving the modern critic's perception that there is a special element of shock in the poems. I share then Miss Tuve's clear affirmative position on the general question "whether historical knowledge is ever aesthetically necessary," but propose that a different selection be made from history in coming at Herbert and the metaphysicals—a selection which tends to confirm rather than deny many of the central findings of their nonhistorical critics.

The Reformation reading of life, as I have perhaps sufficiently stressed, concentrates heavily on shock and surprise. It sees the human situation as paradoxical and improbable in every significant circumstance—that is, in every circumstance relating to salvation—and the ways of God amazing in their contradiction of reasonable expectations. It is devoted, in fact, to exposing the unreasonableness of expectations that man accepts as reasonable and to declaring the exclusive rightness of a version of reality that reason wants to reject. Attention to the goods that reason naturally recommends is self-deception, for the goods of heaven are all that matter. But spiritual ambition is equally mistaken, for the goods of heaven are not to be achieved by human effort or human merit, which can never suffice to make man worthy of heaven's rewards. (Morality is approved for both practical and pious uses, but it is peripheral to the real business of religion. Herbert is a moral poet only in "The Church Porch," on the other side of the wall from "The Church," which treats the urgent questions of God and man.) A recurrent metaphor of commerce underlines the point that man cannot sell himself or his good deeds to God, who sees the self-contamination in the best that man can do (as in the ambitious religious poetry that Herbert deplores in "Jordan" II for the corruption of "weaving myself into the verse"). The moral logic of such commerce is spoiled, however, not only by the tawdriness of the human commodity, but also by God's disinclination to prefer the better to the worse. There is love enough for all in what Herbert, in prose, called "the boundlesse Ocean of God's love, and the unspeakable riches of his loving kindnesse." God might reasonably be expected to hate men as sinful creatures, but he does not.

> As Creatures, he must needs love them; for no perfect Artist ever yet hated his owne worke. As sinfull, he must much more love them; because notwithstanding his infinite hate of sinne, his Love overcame that hate; and with an exceeding great victory, which in the Creation needed not, gave them love for love, even the son of his love out of his bosome of love. So that man, which way soever he turnes, hath two pledges of God's Love . . . the one in his being, the other in his sinfull being: and this as the more faulty in him, so the more glorious in God. [*Works*, p. 283]

There is shock in this simply as a proposition, and the shock of Herbert's poetry is sometimes not a great deal more than that which the repeated proposition supplies. The sixty-three stanzas of "The Sacrifice," for example, are little capsules of Augustinian paradox: Christ on the cross cites the disparity between man's behavior toward God and God's behavior toward man.

> *Oh all ye, who passe by,* whose eyes and minde
> To worldly things are sharp, but to me blinde;

To me, who took eyes that I might you finde:
            Was ever grief like mine?

The greatness of God's grief is, of course, exactly the
measure of His love, the boundless ocean that washes over
sinful man. Miss Tuve points out that the little stanzas
of paradox in the poem have one essential focus: "Man's
blind misreading of the real is behind all the ironies of
this poem, causes that gap between what in truth is, and
how man perceives it."[8] That misreading, however, and
the gap between ostensible truth and the truth of God
is Herbert's constant theme and is the conceptual basis
for a poetic form in which opposites clash violently and
subside in reconciliations which are in fact victories for
one voice in the dialectic and defeats for the other.

"The Collar" exploits the full shock-potential of the
form and demonstrates its precise relationship to the
theological conception—the loose ode structure and the
violence of statement expressing more vividly than Herbert usually attempts to do the terrible unrest of human
self-assertiveness and dramatizing the need for the peace
in God of New Testament promise, for which Calvin
finds such words as "adoption" and "reconciliation" and
which Herbert's loving Father-God conveys in his single
word of admonition, acceptance, and love. The shock and
surprise of such a poem consists largely in its internal col-
lisions, but the blindness which brings man into collision
with God is the universal catastrophe of the human condition, which must not only be depicted in the poem but
assumed in the reader, to be somehow penetrated by the
poet. There is thus a theological rationale for poetic
shock which a poet with Herbert's purposes would not
hesitate to accept. As he declares in the opening stanza

8. *A Reading of George Herbert*, p. 68.

of "The Church Porch," "A verse may finde him, who a sermon flies," and the poet's procedure is not different from his divine master's if he seeks to take the sinner by surprise.

The grandest effects of surprise in metaphysical poetry have a *trompe l'oeil* quality which has suggested affinities with the technical and rhetorical boldness of baroque art and its tendency to deliberate confusion of different orders of reality—as in the "openness," noted in Heinrich Wölfflin's well-known analysis, which eliminates pictorial "framing" elements and confuses the boundaries of picture space and the space in which the viewer stands. Something of the same kind appears to be happening when God breaks into the seemingly closed world of Herbert's poem, or when Vaughan flashes across the infinity separating earth from heaven with the matter-of-fact notation "I saw eternity the other night." Though with more bravura, any number of baroque paintings similarly open heaven to earth in such a way as to induce momentary doubts in the viewer concerning his own astronomical and metaphysical location. Baciccio's ceiling in the Gesu, the principal church of the Jesuits, is a brilliant and flamboyant example: the interior architecture from the clerestory level upward is painted "out" in an immense virtuoso labor of illusionism that puts a rosy-clouded heaven immediately overhead.

Such comparisons perhaps seem to make it possible to assimilate the English metaphysicals to the Catholic baroque, though there are obviously sufficient differences in artistic strategy and general feeling to recommend caution. What can reasonably be said of the aesthetic parallel is that both metaphysical poetry and baroque paintings are intimately tied to the needs of an age of determined religious inwardness in which religious experience acquired an increasingly anti-intellectualist character and

gave increasingly larger importance to the Christian's
affective states. The art that serves religion thus conceived will expectably seek "to surprise, to astonish, to
dazzle,"[9] though it may, of course, use different instruments in different times and places. It is notable, for
example, that the Catholic baroque is splendid and flesh-
ly to an extent obnoxious to the ascetic spirit of Protestantism, which, in fact, expressed itself in some violent
fits of art destruction. One has also to note that Counter-
Reformation Catholic theology does not show these affective, anti-intellectualist tendencies. In Bellarmine, for example, it is conservative, rational, and Thomist. We have
seen, however, in St. Ignatius's *Spiritual Exercises* that
Catholic devotional writing and presumably Catholic
devotional life had an emotional excitement similar to
that which inheres in Protestant ideas of "conversion,"
and it is possible to argue that the essential spirit of post-
Reformation Catholicism is better represented in its popular devotional writers than in its retrospective and offi-
cially defensive theology. Indeed, the religious conscious-
ness of the age, shared by Protestant and Catholic alike,
appears to have been so strongly turned to the devotional
that one may judge (without Protestant bias) that the
theology truest to the time was the devotional theology
of the Reformers, which set aside the infinite variety of
scholasticism to focus with exclusive concentration on the
evangelical nexus of man's intercourse with God.

It is interesting in this regard to consider the evidence
that Helen White and Louis Martz have assembled establishing the acceptability of Catholic devotional literature
to Protestant Englishmen, who were slow to develop
their own. Miss White quotes the Jesuit Robert Parson's

9. E. R. Curtius, "Mannerism," in *European Literature in the
Latin Middle Ages,* trans. Willard R. Trask (New York, 1953), pp.
273–301.

supercilious question to the Anglican Edmund Bunny in
1585 whether "any of his religion did either make or set
forthe (of them selues) any one treatise of this kinde of
subiect? I meane, of deuotion, pietie and contemplation?"
Bunny, hard pressed, claims few purely devotional authors for Protestantism, but can fall back on his theolo-
gians to carry the day: "It cannot be vnknown to you,
but that so many of us as haue written concerning the
institution of a Christian, have effectually handled that
matter [i.e. devotion]. See Calvin thereon in his Institutions. . . . Luther also, in this account, I am sure you
wil grant to be ours."[10]

Affectivity in devotion did not, of course, lead either
the metaphysicals or the Catholic devotional writers to
excesses of individual response such as the mid-seven-
teenth century was to see in the Puritan sectaries. Church
guidance was accepted by both as a necessary control on
idiosyncrasy, and both were concerned to avoid what
John Baptist Saint-Jure, a Jesuit of mystical tendencies
himself, called "the danger of extraordinary ways." To
keep "to the main roads," says Saint-Jure, "is indeed always much safer than straying into remote foot-paths,
even if they are sometimes a bit shorter, because on the
roads there is always someone to keep us from becoming
lost."[11] Herbert takes the same ground in a somewhat
anxious comment on one of *The Hundred and Ten Considerations* of Juan Valdes translated by his friend
Nicholas Ferrar. The Catholic reformer's insistence on
belief "by revelation" needed to be explained as safely
distant from the dangers of enthusiasm: "He often useth
this manner of speech *Beleeving by Revelation, not by*

10. Helen White, *English Devotional Literature, 1600–1640*
(Madison, 1931), pp. 64, 66.
11. Pierre Pourrat, S.S., *Christian Spirituality*, trans. Donald Att-
water (Westminster, Md., 1955), 4: 48.

relation, whereby I understand he meaneth only the effec-
tuall operation or illumination of the holy spirit, testify-
ing, and applying the revealed truth of the Gospell; and
not any private Enthusiasmes, or Revelations" *(Works,*
p. 308).[12]

But Herbert, despite this demur, is in important ways
an enthusiastic poet, and enthusiasm was eventually to
lay claim to him. In 1697 appeared the widely used Dis-
senters' hymnal, *Select Hymns Taken Out of Mr. Herbert's Temple,*[13] which recast thirty-two poems from *The
Temple* in "common metre" for congregational singing,
and John Wesley similarly adapted forty-nine in the
Methodist hymnals which he assembled between 1737
and 1740.[14] George Ryley's exhaustive 1715 manuscript
commentary on all of the poems in *The Temple* was the
labor of one drawn to "the elements in the poems which
the Puritans and later nonconformists found so attractive."[15] No other major poet of the century was so directly useful to nonconformist piety, and one sees immediately the reasons for Herbert's attractiveness. His
account of the religious life, though attentive to church
feasts and occasions and to the church as an institution
having significant procedures and physical characteristics
(in poems omitted in the Dissenting collections) is mainly cast in terms of vivid personal experience which prac-
titioners of individual religion would recognize and appreciate. He appears, in fact, to duplicate in poems the

12. Summers remarks that Herbert "unerringly detected and condemned [Valdes's] exaltation of inspiration above the scriptures, his
quietism, and his implicit anarchism" *(George Herbert,* p. 66).

13. See the Augustan Reprint Society edition, edited by William
E. Stephenson (Los Angeles, 1962).

14. See Elsie A. Leach, "John Wesley's Use of George Herbert,"
Huntington Library Quarterly, 16 (1952): 183–202.

15. Summers, *George Herbert,* p. 59.

essential features of personal history repeated in nonconformist sermons and spiritual autobiographies—the
latter a favorite enthusiastic genre for giving, as a slight-
ly later writer was to say, "a particular Account of Heart-
Occurrences and God's Operations in me."[16]

Herbert not only has heart-occurrences, but, as we have
seen in "The Collar," has the right kind to earn the approval of a Calvinistically based enthusiasm. The all-
important occurrence is, of course, the private revelation
of God's presence and all-sufficing love, as at the end of
"The Collar," or in "The Glance," where, typically, God
embraces man in his worst condition.

> When first thy sweet and gracious eye
>   Vouchsaf'd ev'n in the midst of youth and night
> To look upon me, who before did lie
>   Weltring in sinne;
>   I felt a sugred strange delight,
> Passing all cordials made by any art,
> Bedew, embalme, and overrunne my heart,
>   And take it in.

But the state of mind which precedes these consolations
is of equal interest to enthusiastic Protestantism, which
recorded the surprising motions of the soul in independence of God, "the enslaving motions of an untoward
volition and inclination,"[17] in despairing detail. Herbert
had a no less comprehensive sense of the evils of the self
which the Christian required saving from and no less
wonder at its urgency in going wrong even when it

16. The words are Baxter's, who, however, declined to write
spiritual autobiography on such a plan; see *Reliquae Baxterianae,
Or, Mr. Richard Baxter's Narrative of the Most Memorable Passages of His Life and Times* (1696), p. 124.

17. Samuel Wright, *A Treatise on That Being Born Again Without Which No Man Can be Saved* (New York, 1813), p. 122.

means to go right. The struggling but unregenerate
Augustine is constantly before us.

> For, *I do praise thee, yet I praise thee not:*
> *My prayers mean thee, yet my prayers stray:*
> *I would do well, yet sinne the hand hath got:*
> *My soul doth love thee, yet it loves delay.*
> I cannot skill of these my wayes.
>
> ["Justice," I]

Like Augustine, Herbert could perhaps be said to be
weak in his Christology, yet, with seventeenth-century
Protestantism generally, he bases his faith very strongly
on the promise of the New Testament. And although the
individual's drama of regeneration and redemption tends
to overshadow the drama of Christ's atonement, the incarnation is celebrated as a general instance of the saving process; Christ is God's mercy incarnate vouchsafed
to humankind at large, the public and historical mani-
festation of the grace which operates privately in the
individual soul. His appearance brings a new dispensation as the operation of grace in the soul brings a new
man. Herbert's Christ, like his conception of grace,
gentles and liberalizes Reformation doctrine—especially
as it is represented in Calvin—making both Christ and
grace available to all men. Where the strict Calvinist
might insist on spiritual class distinctions and assign one
soul to bliss and another to damnation on the basis of
"double predestination," Herbert, while not less alert to
distinctions, has more generous notions of divine mercy.
As he says in "Faith," "grace fills up uneven nature," and
this enlarging of the miracle of God's love enters also into
his view of Christ, who brought with him total change
and unconditioned promise—the redemptive "much" of
the second poem entitled "Justice."

O Dreadfull Justice, what a fright and terrour
    Wast thou of old,
    When sinne and errour
  Did show and shape thy looks to me,
  And through their glasse discolour thee!
He that did but look up was proud and bold.

The dishes of thy ballance seem'd to gape,
    Like two great pits;
    The beam and scape
  Did like some torturing engine show;
  Thy hand above did burn and glow,
Danting the stoutest hearts, the proudest wits.

But now that Christs pure vail presents the sight,
    I see no fears:
    Thy hand is white,
  Thy scales like buckets, which attend
  And interchangeably descend,
Lifting to heaven from this well of tears.

For where before thou still didst call on me,
    Now I still touch
    And harp on thee.
  Gods promises have made thee mine;
  Why should I justice now decline?
Against me there is none, but for me much.

                       ["Justice," II]

This trusting and hopeful view of divine intentions
leads Herbert in other poems to typically Protestant ut-
terances of love and joy and gratefulness. The deity thus
addressed is abstract and functional in a way which
Catholic piety would find uninviting, but which fulfills
all Protestant requirements in its promptness of response
to human need and in its swift initiatives. Herbert is in

these poems most hymnlike, and the poem of celebration which begins "My joy, my life, my crown!" is appropriately titled "A True Hymne." But such poems represent the peaks of spiritual assurance, which the Protestant had no expectation of occupying permanently.

> The grosser world stands to thy word and art;
> But thy diviner world of grace
> Thou suddenly dost raise and race,
> And ev'ry day a new Creatour art.
>
> ["The Temper," II]

More often, therefore, God is addressed by a soul oppressed with the weight of its sinfulness and longing for mercy. In some of these, the themes, already glanced at, of despairing self-analysis are dominant, as in "Nature."

> Full of rebellion, I would die,
> Or fight, or travell, or denie
> That thou hast ought to do with me.
>
> O tame my heart;

In others the interest lies in God's attributes rather than man's.

> O let thy height of mercie then
> Compassionate short-breathed men.
>
> ["Repentance"]

In all, the direction of will defines man's spiritual condition, and Herbert in nothing represents Reformation interests and attitudes more clearly than in putting such weight on will. The urgings of the self, according to his constant message, are opposition to God and the means of our destruction. To bend our will in childlike submission to God's is the way of holiness and the condition of grace.

O let me still
Write thee great God, and me a childe:
Let me be soft and supple to thy will . . .
                              ["Holy Baptisme," II]

The Christian's aim should be to have no desires different from God's desires for him, to "aspire to a full con-
sent" ("Discipline"). The position itself in its simplicity,
and its leading corollaries and implicit assumptions in
Reformation doctrine are clustered concentratedly in
"Employment," I.

If as a flowre doth spread and die,
    Thou wouldst extend me to some good,
Before I were by frosts extremitie
                Nipt in the bud;

The sweetnesse and the praise were thine;
    But the extension and the room,
Which in thy garland I should fill, were mine
                At thy great doom.

For as thou dost impart thy grace,
    The greater shall our glorie be.
The measure of our joyes is in this place,
                The stuffe with thee.

Let me not languish then, and spend
    A life as barren to thy praise,
As is the dust, to which that life doth tend,
                But with delaies.

All things are busie; onely I
    Neither bring hony with the bees,
Nor flowres to make that, nor the husbandrie
                To water these.

> I am no link of thy great chain,
> But all my companie is a weed.
> Lord place me in thy consort; give one strain
> To my poore reed.

What speaks most strongly in the poem is the sense of man's entire helplessness and emptiness until helped and filled by God. No spiritual effort is possible for him, no escape from his wretchedness as the useless anomaly in a creation dedicated to function. He is nothing until grace is given and only emerges into significant being as the factor which defines his individuality, his will and self-purpose, is lost in God. Faced logically the situation is a hopeless conundrum, as the mock-logic of "The Hold-fast" makes clear.

> I Threatned to observe the strict decree
> Of my deare God with all my power & might.
> But I was told by one, it could not be;
> Yet I might trust in God to be my light.
> Then will I trust, said I, in him alone.
> Nay, ev'n to trust in him, was also his:
> We must confesse that nothing is our own.
> Then I confesse that he my succour is:
> But to have nought is ours, not to confesse
> That we have nought. I stood amaz'd at this,
> Much troubled, till I heard a friend expresse
> That all things were more ours by being his.

"All my companie is a weed," says "Employment," I: and, if it is transformed into a flower and allowed some good, it is good and belongs to man only insofar as it belongs to God. Thus by the operation of grace is property appalled. If grace is union, however, sin is disunion, and the soul that prays "place me in thy consort; give one strain / To my poore reed" suffers from the sense that there is no harmony in solitary music. The great chain concept is explicitly rejected for man in Herbert's poem; humans are omitted from the ordered associations of the creation. Will has made a breach which only the destruction of the will can close again, and while Herbert and Protestantism are free to contemplate the order and plenitude of the creation in general, their vision of continuity finds a gap at man. This is of course a staggering exception, and it means that when the metaphysical imagination of the seventeenth-century Protestant attends to its primary subject, the relations of man with God and the problems of salvation, it occupies itself with a wholly different framework of ideas and metaphors, those of discontinuity, opposition and conflict—dualism so decided as to have suggested the term "Manichean" to the critics cited earlier.

But the dualism, as we have seen, can be conquered by the action of God's grace and the grace-motivated subjugation of the will.[18] It is a condition in which hope outweighs despair and which, I have argued, leads in poetry to excitements of opposition and reconciliation. In Herbert, it leads to certain other poetic qualities, which criticism has not neglected but which deserve also to be mentioned in the present context. A recent book on Herbert concludes with a paragraph describing his "purity of heart" and "genuine holiness," characteristics which it makes synonymous with humility—the most striking feature of Herbert's tone and one intimately related to his "plain" style.[19] One has no desire to question Herbert's personal saintliness, but the point would

18. L. C. Knights has observed that Herbert's poetry "does not, like some religious poetry, simply express conflict; it is consciously and steadily directed toward resolution and integration" (*Explorations* [London, 1946], p. 121). The point could be made with equal appropriateness of all of the poets treated in this study.

19. Mary Ellen Rickey, *Utmost Art: Complexity in the Verse of George Herbert* (Lexington, Ky., 1966), p. 178.

seem to intrude upon us that humility is a virtue defined
in theology as well as a feature of personality (indeed,
the only virtue to which the Reformation could give
unqualified approval) and that the author of *The Temple* would seek the means in language to commend it.
Its status is unique among Protestant virtues as that
which is enemy to pride and will and self, and is necessarily and self-evidently dumb concerning its own claims
to merit. Moreover, it embraces spiritual states which
Protestant theology identified with precision and which
Herbert's poems fully explicate: (1) the soul's discovery
of its own radical defect and helplessness—the "conviction of sin" which is the initial process of regeneration,
and (2) the condition of "righteousness," conceived as a
reconciliation with God in which will and the claims of
self are surrendered. Herbert is especially the poet of
that surrender. As Miss Tuve has finely said, he is committed to "the immolation of the individual will" and
his poems are "acts of submission."[20]

The implications of this attitude for poetic style are
clear. Despite his virtuoso mastery of his art and his
manifest pleasure in artifice, Herbert will be plain. Plainness may, of course, have been legislated by other considerations than simply the need to put down will. Ruth
Wallerstein and others would put us in mind that Augustine had rhetorical as well as theological importance to
seventeenth-century poets and that a long tradition de-
scending from Augustine prescribed a low style in preaching.[21] But Herbert seems to give his reasons fully in the

20. *A Reading of George Herbert*, p. 195.
21. Ruth C. Wallerstein, *Studies in Seventeenth-Century Poetic*
(Madison, 1930), pp. 27–30. Summers discusses very fully the relation
of Herbert's plainness with his preacherly necessities. I do not take
issue with Summers's conclusions, though I have thought it more
important in my own discussion of the matter to emphasize connections with theological attitudes; see *George Herbert*, pp. 95–119.

second "Jordan" poem where, in a series of brilliant and striking images, he deplores fancy effects in religious verse as contaminations of self.

> Thousands of notions in my brain did runne,
> Off'ring their service, if I were not sped:
> I often blotted what I had begunne;
> This was not quick enough, and that was dead.
> Nothing could seem too rich to clothe the sunne,
> Much lesse those joyes which trample on his head.
>
> As flames do work and winde, when they ascend,
> So did I weave my self into the sense.

The plain style, on the other hand, works the self out, and that overthrow and submission—with no concessions to the idea of progress or improvement—was, of course, a basic Reformation project.

5 Marvell and Vaughan: The Psalm Model of Reconciliation

The increasing study of hermetic and Platonic aspects of Marvell's poetry and appreciation of his delicate political equilibrism have tended to shift attention away from his Reformation attitudes, which were thought conspicuous, however, by earlier readers to whom Marvell seemed plainly enough the second-ranking Puritan poet of England. Certainly, to his contemporaries his theological position needed no explaining. He was known, for example, as the author of a defense of Bishop Croft (who had declared, while arguing against the authority of the Church Fathers in general, that "There is no man I ever heard of or read of to whom I could more readily submit than to St. Austin"),[1] and he had scolded Samuel Parker in *The Rehearsal Transpros'd* for (among other faults of argument and character) undervaluing divine grace and making "a constant pissing-place" of John Calvin's grave.[2] It would be difficult not to agree with

1. *The Naked Truth, or the True State of the Primitive Church,* By an Humble Moderator (1675), p. 13.

2. "Mr. Smirke, or the Divine in Mode," in *The Complete Works of Andrew Marvell,* ed. Alexander G. Grosart (1873), 3: 45.

John Wallace that the more one contemplates the "core of actual belief" in Marvell's religion, "the firmer the outlines become of his moderate Calvinism, his aversion to the hierarchy of the Church of England, and his concurrence in most of the principles of nonconformity."[3] To be sure, these are not the only outlines traceable in the poems, but they appear strongly in some, entitling Marvell to at least brief consideration as a poet of grace.

"The Coronet" is a poem full of Herbertian reminiscences, using some of the same contrasting image pairs as "The Collar" and a Herbert-like speaker who "personalizes" a spiritual predicament—the only such speaker in Marvell's handful of religious lyrics. Its theme is that of "Jordan" II—the contaminations of self that spoil man's efforts to perform a work which will be worth offering to God.

> When for the Thorns with which I long, too long,
>   With many a piercing wound,
>   My Saviours head have crown'd,
> I seek with Garlands to redress that Wrong:
>   Through every Garden, every Mead,
> I gather flow'rs (my fruits are only flow'rs)
>   Dismantling all the fragrant Towers
> That once adorn'd my Shepherdesses head.
> And now when I have summ'd up all my store,
>   Thinking (so I my self deceive)
>   So rich a Chaplet thence to weave
> As never yet the king of Glory wore:
>   Alas I find the Serpent old
>   That, twining in his speckled breast,
>   About the flow'rs disguis'd does fold,
>   With wreaths of Fame and Interest.

3. *Destiny His Choice: The Loyalism of Andrew Marvell* (Cambridge, 1968), p. 193.

Ah, foolish Man, that wouldst debase with them,
And mortal Glory, Heavens Diadem!
But thou who only could'st the Serpent tame,
Either his slipp'ry knots at once untie,
And disintangle all his winding Snare:
Or shatter too with him my curious frame:
And let these wither, so that he may die,
Though set with Skill and chosen out with Care.
That they, while Thou on both their Spoils dost tread,
May crown thy Feet, that could not crown thy Head.[4]

Pierre Legouis has written of the "Calvinism" of "The Coronet" but seems to mean by the term no more than that the poem expresses a general "Puritan mistrust of profane ornaments, even when presented to the Creator."[5] It is, of course, a thoroughly Protestant poem, embodying much more essential Protestant attitudes than Legouis identifies. Its anti-aestheticism is an incidental feature of a theology—in contact with the poem at every point—which asserts the disastrousness of human effort in conciliating God. God's favor is not to be purchased by anything that man can offer—human offerings at best falling pathetically short of the value of the favor requested ("my fruits are only flow'rs") and inescapably flawed with self-interest. The choice is not open to us to cease our "wounding" of the savior, and the purpose to "redress that wrong," for all its apparent piety, is a mistaken assertion of human adequacy in a field where human claims should not intrude. The rich chaplet of line 11 is said to be one such "As never yet the king of Glory wore" not merely in hyperbolic description of the fineness of the gift, but because of the impossibility of un-

---

4. *The Poems and Letters of Andrew Marvell*, ed. H. M. Margoliouth (Oxford, 1927), 1: 14.
5. *Andrew Marvell: Poet, Puritan, Patriot* (Oxford, 1965), p. 37.

assisted man adding to God's satisfactions, or, indeed, of
returning anything but ill for God's good. The speckled
serpent is in all we do, however complete its disguises and
however determined our self-deceptions. J. B. Leishman's
suggested rewriting of the last lines of the poem so as,
apparently, to let the flowers fare somewhat better at
Christ's feet than the serpent misses the point.[6] Serpent
and flowers are inseparable and suffer the same fate; the
forward self spoils our best acts, and its correction is the
necessary work of grace. That we should credit ourselves
with "skill" and "care" in doing shows exactly the limitations of the human perspective as it bears on justification,
for the more satisfactorily we appear to be doing on our
own, the more certainly we cut ourselves off from
Providence.

"On a Drop of Dew" fits much less neatly than "The
Coronet" into the pattern of the Augustinian poem. It
teases out its conceit without pretense of personal involvement, without, in fact, any representation of self for the
Augustinian drama to take place in or against. It separates
soul and body in a style more Platonist than Christian—
and directly contrary to the Augustinian teaching which
refused to except the soul from the blame for human
corruption. The Soul's exclusion of the world (line 29)
while receiving the "Day" of divine attention is not more
characteristic of Augustinism than of any other variety
of Christianity, nor are the emotions of disdain and love
which attend these processes. One is tempted to claim a
shadow of Augustinian significance for the play of op-

6. *The Art of Marvell's Poetry* (London, 1966), p. 196:
   And let them wither, so that he may die,
   These flow'rs, though set with skill and culled with care,
   That they, while Thou on him and them dost tread,
   May crown thy Feet, that could not crown thy Head.

posite attitudes in the poem as it withdraws from the things of the world while responding also to the pull of their attractiveness. Likewise the striking last lines describe a return to God managed wholly, as in the conception of Augustine and the Reformers, by divine energy: their neo-Platonic look—the cyclic and vertical flow of being—seems to become fair Augustinism when the sun of the last line is identified with the sun in the middle of the poem, which does not merely absorb what flows up to it but fosters the flowing process with its warmth and pity.

A much more clearly Augustinian view of the soul's responsibility for sin appears in "A Dialogue between the Soul and Body," where the body is allowed to complain wittily of the "ill Spirit" that possesses it. It is the soul that produces the "Palsie Shakes of Fear," the "hidden Ulcer" of hatred, the twin madnesses of Joy and Sorrow and the theological grievance stated in the body's final rhetorical question: "What but a Soul could have the wit / To build me up for Sin so fit?" Marvell here occupies the same theological ground as the "mortalist" Milton, who could see no justice in exempting the soul from the cost of sin or postponing its forfeits. For both poets, as for a most ancient tradition of Christian thought, the rational and voluntary part of man participated as fully as the body in what St. Paul termed, collectively, "the flesh." One may take exception, therefore, to H. R. Swardson's view that Marvell's poem argues for "bodily innocence" (that sin lives principally in reason and will does not necessarily imply innocence in the body) and thus embodies "a conception of the natural that, to some extent, works *against* the religious tradition."[7] One can reach this conclusion only by defining "the religious tradi-

7. *Poetry and the Fountain of Light* (London, 1962), p. 94.

tion" in such a way as to exclude the tradition of Paul, Augustine, and the Reformation.

"A Dialogue between the Soul and Body" is a poem of symmetrical oppositions in which no conclusive resolution is reached, unless one makes more than fair allowance for the fact that Body has the last word. Marvell's other poem in this interesting subgenre, "A Dialogue between the Resolved Soul and Created Pleasure," is managed quite differently. It portrays an unequal conflict between an unconvincing seducer (who offers a temptation for each of the five senses and appeals additionally to the vanities of wealth, power, and learning) and a secure soul that turns away each temptation with an answer that Bunyan would have called "snibbish." To six lines of ingratiating welcome by Pleasure it responds: "I sup above, and cannot stay / To bait so long upon the way." Invited to voluptuary rest, it answers with the prim self-approval which is its constant style: "My gentler Rest is on a Thought, / Conscious of doing what I ought." Its assurance is that of the "right" voice in the dialogue, and its rightness is never challenged; the poem marches by planned advances to a resolution in which the "Resolved Soul" takes all. In Murray Krieger's terms, the "cards have been stacked," and the collision of opposites is an obvious "manipulation" designed mainly to enhance the satisfactions of calm when the poem finally reaches the stage of reconciliation.

It is worth noting that the reconciliation is conceived in what we may now perhaps describe as "classical" Augustinian terms. The soul in its last speech rejects any of the possible roads which the mind might, on its own, choose to take to God. Pleasure has offered such knowledge as can "Try what depth the Centre draws; / And then to Heaven climb," and the Soul responds: "None thither mounts by the degree / Of Knowledge, but Hu-

mility." The resolved soul, absolute for God, can only
be so by the systematic neglect of every claim of self. It
is only self, in fact, which recognizes "degree," and one
is brought back again to Cassirer's comment on the
machinery of "graduated mediation" which diminished
transcendence and reduced the burden of the "inconceivable" for the rationalist theology of the late Middle
Ages (see p. 44, above). The "humility" of Reformation
theology sees no degrees, but only the appalling distance
that separates fallen man from God.

That distance is closed in "Bermudas," where Marvell
describes a condition of blessedness in nature. The poem
has resemblances, as Margoliouth and others have noted,
to the exotic natural description of John Smith's *General
History of Virginia* and to Waller's "The Battle of the
Summer Islands." But the differences are at least as
striking. The first canto of Waller's poem has seemed a
source for Marvell's especially in the following passage:

> Bermuda, walled with rocks, who does not know?
> That happy island where huge lemons grow,
> And orange trees, which golden fruit do bear,
> The Hesperian garden boasts of none so fair;
> Where shining pearl, coral, and many a pound
> On the rich shore, of ambergris is found.[8]

This shares with "Bermudas" a clustering richness of
natural things, but lacks the attention to means which
gives Marvell's poem theological interest. ("Nature,"
some lines farther on, is the only responsible agent cited.)
In "Bermudas" the fruits and ambergris are found where
they are in consequence of the direct action of Providence,
and what is wonderful about them is the force with which

8. *Poetical Works of Edmund Waller,* ed. Robert Bell (London,
n.d.), p. 97.

they represent to the prayerful and regenerate exiles God's miraculous intervention in nature on their behalf.[9] The poem describes a harmony achieved only by the action of divine grace.

> He gave us this eternal Spring,
> Which here enamells every thing;
> And sends the Fowl's to us in care,
> On daily Visits through the Air.
> He hangs in shades the Orange bright,
> Like golden Lamps in a green Night.

Compared with this, Waller gives us a stage set, but no chief actor, or, really, a different play. Parallels to Marvell's play are better to be sought in literature which celebrates actions of divine grace making harmony between creature and creator. Such parallels can, in fact, be found everywhere in seventeenth-century religious literature, the work of those (sometimes millenarian) "seekers of Eden" who, as Helen White has suggested, carry the Reformation retreat from the medieval church to the primitive church several steps farther—"back into the days when no church was needed, . . . the unbroken

9. Despite some difficulty in terms, I am in essential agreement with Harold E. Tolliver's reading of the poem as an imagining of "history redeemed by providence" (*Marvell's Ironic Vision* [New Haven, 1965], pp. 100–03). While, of course, agreeing that Marvell's poetry exhibits "ironic" structures, or patterns of opposition, I am not able to share Tolliver's general view of the sources of Marvell's ironic vision, nor his sense of the issues which engaged it. Consider, for example, the suggestion that "self-definition is almost exclusively for Marvell a product of combat against exterior nature. Hence art rather than grace tends to become his chief mode of realizing the soul's self-sufficiency and of imposing order upon nature" (p. 17). This suggestion is scarcely intelligible in the perspective of Augustinian attitudes concerning grace and the self.

communion of Eden."[10] Marvell's "The Garden" similarly celebrates this communion and clearly derives from
the same scriptural prototypes, among which should be
included the landscape of Psalms as well as the Eden of
Genesis.

The first act of God's grace was to create nature, whose
responsiveness to divine command is imaged in the miraculous vitality of the landscape in Genesis.

> And God said, Let the earth bring forth grass, the
> herb yielding seed, and the fruit tree yielding fruit
> after his kind, whose seed is in itself, upon the earth:
> and it was so. / And the earth brought forth grass,
> and herb yielding seed after his kind, and the tree
> yielding fruit, whose seed was in itself, after his
> kind: and God saw that it was good. . . . And God
> made two great lights; the greater light to rule the
> day, and the lesser light to rule the night: he made
> the stars also. / And God set them in the firmament
> of the heaven to give light upon the earth, / And to
> rule over the day and over the night, and to divide
> the light from the darkness: and God saw that it was
> good. [Gen. 1:11–18][11]

It is not fanciful, I think, to claim to find amid what
seems to be Marvell's several recollections of this scene
some borrowed beams of the sun and moon of Genesis
in Bermuda's orange groves. "He hangs in shades the
Orange bright, / Like golden Lamps in a green Night."

---

10. *The Metaphysical Poets* (New York, 1936), p. 275. Bermuda as
Eden was not a notion original with Marvell. See Rosalie Colie,
"Bermudas and the Puritan Paradise," *Renaissance News*, 10 (1957):
75–79.

11. Here and elsewhere I quote from the King James version of
the Bible.

God's active presence in nature in symbol of reconciliation with man is a feature of "the Psalmist's" message
also, and contributes to the peculiar status of Psalms as
the book of the Old Testament that most clearly anticipates the promise of divine love and redemption in the
New. George Wither remarked in *A Preparation to the
Psalter* (1619) that it was a "compendium of both Testa-
ments" (p. 64) and so essential for its consolations that
"No one Booke of all the holy Scriptures is so many
wayes comfortably necessary for a Christian: none so
plainly or particularly mentioned those things which
concerne the mysteries of our Redemption" (p. 127). A
modern commentary begins by noting that the very first
word of the first psalm is a word of comfort—"Blessed is
the man . . . ," a tone which the Psalter characteristically
maintains through its various hymns of praise and thanks-
giving and even its laments.[12] Wither finds in it "a
precious balme for every present sore and a preservative
against all future disenchantment . . . a means of comfort
and hope of recovery" (p. 127). There is "no other book,"
said Calvin, "in which there is recorded so many deliver-
ances," nor one which gives such prominence to "the
evidences and experiences of the fatherly providence and
solicitude which God exercises towards us."[13]

What is most noteworthy about the psalms, however,
as a background to Marvell's poem is their special perspective on the divine, which leaves its awful transcendence
undiminished while imagining its intimate and solicitous
connection with man in nature.[14] The God of Psalms

12. Artur Weiser, *The Psalms: A Commentary,* 5th ed., trans.
Herbert Hartwell (Philadelphia, 1959), p. 102.
13. *Commentary on the Book of Psalms,* vol. 1, trans. James Ander-
son (Edinburgh, 1845), p. xxxviii.
14. The interplay and mixture of God's transcendence and presence in the psalms is usefully discussed in Wallace I. Wolverton's

is not merely a loving God, but one who loves miraculously, transforming Nature's ordinary appearances and operations into the efficient vehicles of his benevolençe. He walks only on magic landscapes—where, typically, in the most famous of the psalms, among green pastures and still waters, "he restoreth my soul." Other passages are still more notably consistent with Marvell's imagining, as the following from Psalm 147:

> . . . sing praise upon the harp unto our God: / Who covereth the heaven with clouds, who prepareth rain for the earth, who maketh grass to grow upon the mountains. / He giveth to the beast his food, and to the young ravens which cry. . . . Praise thy God, O Zion. / For he hath strengthened the bars of thy gates; he hath blessed thy children within thee. / He maketh peace in thy borders, and filleth thee with the finest of the wheat.

Or this from Psalm 65:

> . . . O God of our salvation; who art the confidence of all the ends of the earth, and of them that are afar off upon the sea: / Which by his strength setteth fast the mountains; being girded with power: /

---

article, "The Psalmists' Belief in God's Presence," *Canadian Journal of Theology,* 9 (1963): 82–94. See also George S. Gunn's discussion of the "nature psalms" in *God in the Psalms* (Edinburgh, 1956). Discussion of the influence of the psalms in English poetry has centered on Herbert. See Louis L. Martz, *The Poetry of Meditation,* 2d ed. (New Haven, 1962), pp. 273–82; Harold Fisch, *Jerusalem and Albion: The Hebraic Factor in Seventeenth-Century Poetry* (London, 1964), pp. 56–65; Heather Asals, "The Voice of George Herbert's 'The Church' " *ELH,* 36 (1969): 511–28. Lily B. Campbell in *Divine Poetry and Drama in Sixteenth-Century England* (Cambridge, 1959) traces psalm influence in the previous century in a movement of divine poetry against profane.

Which stilleth the noise of the seas, the noise of their
waves, and the tumult of the people. / They also
that dwell in the uttermost parts are afraid at thy
tokens: thou makest the outgoings of the morning
and evening to rejoice. / Thou visitest the earth, and
waterest it: thou greatly enrichest it with the river of
God, which is full of water: thou preparest them
corn, when thou hast so provided for it. / Thou
waterest the ridges thereof abundantly: thou settlest
the furrows thereof: thou makest it soft with showers:
thou blessest the springing thereof. / Thou crownest
the year with thy goodness; and thy paths drop
fatness. / They drop upon the pastures of the wilderness: and the little hills rejoice on every side. / The
pastures are clothed with flocks; the valleys also are
covered with corn; they shout for joy, they also sing.

Some possible echoes of a more specific kind include
the fowl which, in "Bermudas," God "sends to us in
care," repeating the favor shown Israel when "He rained
flesh upon them as dust, and feathered fowls like as the
sand of the sea" (Ps. 78:27). Compare also Psalm 105:40,
"The people asked also, and he brought quails and satisfied
them with the bread of heaven." Similarly, Marvell's
Sea-Monster probably owes something to the Leviathan
of Psalm 104:27. But such resemblances in detail are less
suggestive than the shared perspective on man and God.
Marvell's "Bermudas" and many of the psalms seem to
belong to a special subcategory of "poetry of reconciliation," in which the whole action of the poems is reconciling, with no preliminary clash of opposites, no allowance
given to the independent tendencies of the human will.
God and man share a single impulse, and entire poems
elaborate the mood of the moment when the speaker in
Herbert's "The Collar" hears the divinely spoken word

"Child"—in that poem the surprising climax of a long contest of will. That this psalm mode, though more even-tenored and directly consoling, equally reflects the sense of dualism and division which we have studied elsewhere, and that it spoke to the Reformation of this condition (with its cure), can be shown in the psalm commentaries which the period produced in abundance. Here is Calvin on Psalm 8:4 ("What is man, that thou art mindful of him"):

> It is, indeed, a wonderful thing that the Creator of heaven, whose glory is so surpassingly great as to ravish us with the highest admiration, condescends so far as graciously to take upon him the care of the human race. . . . We see that miserable men, in moving upon the earth, are mingled with the vilest creatures; and therefore, God, with very good reason, might despise them and reckon them of no account; if he were to stand upon the consideration of his own greatness or dignity. The prophet, therefore, speaking interrogatively abases their condition, intimating that God's wonderful goodness is displayed the more brightly in that so glorious a Creator, whose majesty shines resplendently in the heavens, graciously condescends to adorn a creature so miserable and vile as man is with the greatest glory, and to enrich him with numberless blessings. . . . Whoever, therefore, is not astonished and deeply affected at this miracle, is more than ungrateful and stupid.[15]

English poetry of the seventeenth century gives evidence that its makers were indeed affected by this miracle and that they found the Book of Psalms variously useful as a model for dealing with it. That this was a Reforma-

15. *Commentary on the Book of Psalms*, 1: 100–01.

tion phenomenon scarcely needs arguing. The Reformers testify massively to the congeniality of the psalms to Reformation thinking (a congeniality similarly felt by Augustine, who in this also prepared for later developments). And it is obvious that the psalms became available as an influence on poetry in a new and more forceful way as the Reformation took up the cause of Scripture against the Church, insisting that the Bible was the only authoritative source of truth for Christians and making that truth available in the great vernacular translations. Luther enlisted the poets of Germany in the production of a German Psalter, and psalm translation quickly became established as an important poetic sideline in England. Douglas Bush describes the "overwhelming flood of metrical versions of the complete Psalter or of selected psalms."[16] In these circumstances it would seem inevitable that poets should accept the psalms as models for their own practice in divine poetry and "the Psalmist" as a major predecessor.

VAUGHAN

Henry Vaughan is not in every way the natural sharer of a chapter with Marvell. For although he also has been shown to be accessible, in fact more than Marvell, to hermetic and Platonic interpretation, his religious and political connections, such as they were, put him in an opposite camp, and differences of temper, sensibility, and experience are immediately obvious. He shares a taste for landscape animated with divine presence, however, which results in some passages having the psalmlike features just glanced at in "Bermudas" and which Louis Martz has shown to derive from the "Augustinian seeker's" sense of the blessedness of created things.[17] "Religion" begins

16. *English Literature in the Earlier Seventeenth Century,* 2d ed. (Oxford, 1962), p. 73.
17. *The Paradise Within,* pp. 17–31.

"My God, when I walke in those groves, / And leaves thy spirit doth still fan."[18] The most brilliant stanza of "Regeneration" owes its richness to visual expansion of this conceit of divine presence and transformation:

> The unthrift Sunne shot vitall gold
> A thousand peeces,
> And heaven its azure did unfold
> Checqur'd with snowie fleeces,
> The aire was all in spice

"The Search" imagines the wilderness metamorphosed in Christ's forty days' habitation.

> With Seraphins there talked he
> His fathers flaming ministrie,
> He heav'nd their *walks,* and with his eyes
> Made those wild shades a Paradise,
> Thus was the desert sanctified
> To be the refuge of his bride.

But Vaughan's almost compulsively repeated image of reconciliation between God and man is not this ecstatically visualized landscape. It is silence, often preceded by noise: "loud, evil days" ("The Night"), "False *Ecchoes,* and Confused sounds" ("Religion"). God comes in quiet; indeed, his reconciliation with man is quietness itself.

> Gods silent, searching flight:
> When my Lords head is fill'd with dew, and all
> His locks are wet with the clear drops of night;
> His still, soft call;
> His knocking time; The souls dumb watch.
>   ["The Night"]

18. *The Complete Poetry of Henry Vaughan,* ed. French Fogle (New York, 1965), p. 148. Citations of Vaughan's poems are to this edition.

Robert Ellrodt has described Vaughan's longing for "un univers où règne le calme. La vague sans repos et bruyante du temps s'y apaise, avant de mourir sur la grève de l'éternité."[19]

The private and personal qualities of Vaughan's sensibility do not, however, obscure the fact that he drew deeply on the Augustinian conceptions which the age made available and gave them full play in the structural dynamics of his poetry. The first poem of *Silex Scintillans* is "Regeneration," which employs a title already hallowed by Herbert's use and treats what we have seen to be the essential and dominant theme of Augustinian-Protestant spirituality.

The narrative pattern of the poem is that of Augustinian biography with Bunyanesque embellishments and reminiscences of Herbert. It begins with the identification of a spiritual condition which is perhaps not simply, as George Williamson has recently written, that of being "a ward of the world as opposed to God, and still in bonds to sin."[20]

> A Ward, and still in bonds, one day
> I stole abroad,

19. *Les Poètes Métaphysiques Anglais* (Paris, 1960), 1. ii. 205.

20. *Six Metaphysical Poets* (New York, 1967), p. 187. Ross Garner, beginning like Williamson and most other commentators on the poem, with the supposition that the bonds represent captivity to sin, raises the question whether Vaughan is identifying sin with the law. "Did Vaughan, then, intend to contrast the Old Testament dispensation of the law with the New Testament dispensation of Grace and the glorious liberty of the children of God (Rom. 8:21)?" (*Henry Vaughan: Experience and the Tradition* [Chicago, 1959], p. 51). Although this possibility does not appear to enter importantly into Garner's interpretation of the poem, it should of course be recognized that the contrast of dispensations, the analogue in the world's history to regeneration in the individual soul, will echo inescapably in any poem on the latter subject.

It was high-spring, and all the way
   Primros'd, and hung with shade;
Yet, was it frost within,
      And surly winds
Blasted my infant buds, and sinne
   Like Clouds ecclips'd my mind.

The poem can be seen as a somewhat rambling and un-compressed variation on the theme of Herbert's "The Collar," which it echoes closely in its first lines (almost matching its second line word for word), and Herbert's speaker, of course, protests at his bondage to God, not to the world. "Ward" in Vaughan's poem has at least over-tones of "protective custody," a different thing from penal servitude, and one can find a counterpart to his "bonds" in Herbert's rope of sands, constraining obedi-ence to God: "Which pettie thoughts have made, and made to thee / Good cable, to enforce and draw, / And be thy law." A main reason, however, for urging the possibil-ity that wardship for Vaughan here means the service of God rather than the world is that it seems to make poor sense to describe a man in bondage to the world stealing abroad to enter it. What we appear to have here, instead, as in "The Collar," is a typical Augustinian restaging of the primal act of disobedience. Man turns to the world and away from God, opposing his will to God's and allow-ing bad love (that which is characteristic of Augustine's earthly city) to take the place in him of good.

Delight in the world is short-lived as he discovers that the apparent blessedness of his new freedom is a cheat when claimed by the self in independence of God. Man's true condition, thus situated, is a "frost within," and the speaker of Vaughan's poem comes quickly to the recogni-tion that the consequence of his act is a devastation. He has "stolen abroad," furtively and guiltily abandoning

his true good, turning the course of his life—"My walke"
—into a "monstrous mountain'd thing." The recognition
is of course itself a useful event in the process of regeneration, corresponding to that "humiliation," "contrition,"
or "conviction of sin" which is a frequent initial step in
conversion. In fact, for some writers on the subject, it is
a necessity that "desolations" precede the "consolations"
of achieved conversion, however that precondition is
brought about. (John Cotton states the position held in
Massachusetts: "If the Lord mean to save you, He will
rend, as it were, the caul from the heart . . . when the
heart and will is broken.")[21]

Thus broken, Vaughan's pilgrim "sighs upwards,"
painfully reaching a pinnacle emblematically provided
with a pair of scales which weigh his merits and demerits
and show the insufficiency of the former.

> 'Twixt steps, and falls
> I reach'd the pinacle, where plac'd
> I found a paire of scales,
> I tooke them up and layd
> In th'one late paines,
> The other smoake, and pleasures weigh'd
> But prov'd the heavier graines.

The allegory is not obscure at this point, and its message
is the familiar one of Augustinian Christianity.[22] Having

21. *A Treatise of the Covenant of Grace,* quoted in Norman Pettit,
The Heart Prepared: Grace and Conversion in Puritan Spiritual Life
(New Haven, 1966), p. 129.

22. E. C. Pettit finds Vaughan's scales a difficult inversion of a
common emblem whose accustomed use is to "demonstrate the
worthless lightness of the things of the world, etc., balanced against
the substantial weights of spiritual things" *(Of Paradise and Light:
A Study of Vaughan's Silex Scintillans* [Cambridge, 1960], p. 107).
The difficulty would seem to be a good deal reduced, however, and
the inversion reversed if we see that Vaughan is taking the orthodox

arrived at a sense of the seriousness of his sin and need of
regeneration, the Pilgrim has taken to the first resort of
natural man, self-help. His climb to the peak is an un-
ambiguous symbol of the mistaken human aspiration to
achieve salvation by human means. The "pains" of moral
effort, of course, lack the necessary weight, and he is commanded "Away!" to a succession of emblematic scenes
showing the action of grace, with emphasis on its inex-
haustibility, the wonder of its choices, and its indifference
to the requirements of natural reason: it goes "where it
pleases."

Vaughan perhaps shows a similar indifference in the
arrangement of episodes in the last half of the poem.
There seems no clear reason, for example, why the "new
spring" announced in line 38 and described and expanded
in the following stanza could not suffice as an adequate
symbol of regeneration. Line 40, "The unthrift Sunne
shot vitall gold," seems to say almost all that logic requires
(Grace is given unthriftily, indeed with infinite generosity; it comes suddenly and without warning—"shot"; and
what it gives is the gift of true and transformed life—
"vitall gold"), and the remaining lines of the stanza, at
once profuse and delicate, beautifully satisfying each
bodily sense, would seem to render the new spring with
the necessary imaginative particularity. The allegory goes
on, however, shifting away somewhat from an account
of the speaker's own spiritual condition, but not depart-
ing from the themes of Reformation Augustinism. First,
the stones of the fountain introduce the matter of special
election (some stones pass through the water to salvation,
while others—in a strikingly inverted crucifixion image—
"nail'd to the Center stood"). The problem is returned

Reformation position on the futility of works in the process of
salvation.

to in the next stanza, for no other reason apparently than to complete the catalogue of scriptural symbols made contact with in the title and trailing verse from the Song of Solomon ("Arise O North, and come thou South-wind, and blow upon my garden, that the spices thereof may flow out"). Some flowers sleep while others "take in the Ray," but when the wind of regeneration enters in the last stanza, it does not seem to come near either, instead acting out another independent episode, tied only thematically to what has preceded it.

The poem seems to suffer from an allegorical overplus, a purpose expansive in the manner of Bunyan, but expressed in a form not suited to such expansions. In fact, however, there is less wasted motion than may appear. The last four stanzas depict not merely a series of emblems of grace, but (with no less interest from the standpoint of Augustinian theology) the soul's perplexity among them. The mind and senses tire with the effort to understand, but persist with anxious questions, wondering, desiring, musing, listening, turning, seeking. They are answered eventually with a response which is at once less and more than they ask.

> But while I listning sought
>   My mind to ease
> By knowing, where 'twas, or where not,
>   It whisper'd; *Where I please.*

"Where I please" is, in rational terms, a nonanswer, a response remarkable for its contradiction of the spirit in which the questions are asked. But it is also an assurance, similar to his sudden appearance at the end of "The Collar," of God's active presence and good will. Its effect on Vaughan's questioner is much the same as on Herbert's: questions cease, rational inquiry aimed at the knowledge of God and understanding of his way is

suddenly overwhelmed by the *experience* of the divine
presence and instant surrender to it: "Lord, then said I,
On me one breath, / And let me dye before my death!"

The debate concerning Vaughan's status as a "mystic"
seems oblique to the main question in such a poem as
"Regeneration"; so, to a lesser degree, does Ross Garner's
description of the poem as Vaughan's own "spiritual
autobiography," embodying his special kind of religious
experience—"a longing for incorporation into the dark
night of the soul."[23] Garner argues for a distinction
between "theological" and "religious" (or devotional)
poems and claims "Regeneration" for the latter class—a
poetic response to truths assented to as "real things, . . .
images derived from experience, . . . data provided by the
senses and imagination," not as abstractions or "notions"
divorced from personal experience. If the distinction is
accepted, Garner's assignment of "Regeneration" to the
religious kind would seem to be right, though it should
be clear from our examination that the poem exposes no
uniquely personal aspects of religious experience; it follows in detail a pattern which we have recognized as
typical of Reformation piety and which is specified in
Reformation theology. Indeed, while one can imagine
a considerable usefulness for Garner's distinction in a
different period in literary history, it is misleading as
applied to poets whose roots are in Reformation Christianity. For the Reformation, of course, aimed exactly at such
alterations in spirituality as would bring theology and
devotion together: its theology describes and demands
devotional experience, and its characteristic devotional
experience conforms to the description of its theology. One
can maintain then that Vaughan's "Regeneration" is a
theological poem, without casting doubt on the ultimate
authenticity for the poet of the experience it reports:

23. *Henry Vaughan*, p. 153.

Vaughan need not have gone through "conversion" himself (although it is likely that he did) to know the Protestant drama of the soul in vivid detail and assent to it feelingly.

We have seen that drama abridged in poems of psalm-like communion, and we have seen it somewhat softened and abstracted in the allegorical narrative of "Regeneration." Vaughan, like most of his contemporaries, can imagine it as violent collision, however, and appears, indeed, to propose it in its starkest and most violent form as the subject of *Silex Scintillans.* His explanation of the emblem of the heart of flint on his 1650 title page seems to promise that the poems to follow will produce horrific excitements, in the style of Donne's *Holy Sonnets,* from the clash of human and divine wills:

> You plan to conquer force by force. You launch your attack and shatter that boulder, my stony heart. What was stone, becomes flesh. Look at it, broken in pieces! Look, its fragments are flashing at last to heaven and to you, and my cheeks are wet with tears wrung from flint.[24]

In fact, such excitements do occur in the poems, and it is clear that they represent an aspect of grace to which Vaughan's imagination was fully responsive.

> My God, how gracious art thou! I had slipt
> > Almost to hell,
> And on the verge of that dark, dreadful pit
> > Did hear them yell,
> But O thy love! thy rich, almighty love
> > That sav'd my soul,
> > > ["The Relapse"]

24. "Authoris (de se) Emblema," translated in *Complete Poetry of Henry Vaughan,* p. 137.

The infernal setting in this poem is unique in Vaughan,
but not the sense of sharp reversals, either accomplished
or wished for.

O Knit me, that am crumbled dust! the heape
                    Is all dispers'd, and cheape;
              Give for a handfull, but a thought
                              And it is bought;
                                    Hadst thou
Made me a starre, a pearle, or a rain-bow,
                    The beames I then had shot
                    My light had lessend not,
                              But now
I find my selfe the lesse, the more I grow;
                              The world
Is full of voices; Man is call'd, and hurl'd
                    By each, he answers all,
                    Knows ev'ry note, and call,
                              Hence, still
Fresh dotage tempts, or old usurps his will.
Yet, hadst thou clipt my wings, when Coffin'd in
                    This quicken'd masse of sinne,
              And saved that light, which freely thou
                    Didst then bestow,
                                    I feare
I should have spurn'd, and said thou didst forbeare;
                    Or that thy store was lesse,
                    But now since thou didst blesse
                              So much,
I grieve, my God! that thou hast made me such.
                              I grieve?
O, yes! thou know'st I doe; Come, and releive
              And tame, and keepe downe with thy light
              Dust that would rise, and dimme my sight,
                    Lest left alone too long

> Amidst the noise, and throng,
>   Oppressed I
> Striving to save the whole, by parcells dye.
>   ["Distraction"]

There are notable echoes here of Donne's "Goodfriday, 1613. Riding Westward," though one observes that Vaughan's treatment of *distraction* (i.e. deviation from the way indicated by God's will) softens drama toward reflectiveness. He has, of course the essential Reformation view of man as "the gourd of sin and sorrow," and he understands sin according to Reformation definitions: "Wilful rebellions, and suppressions" ("Repentance")— a constant framework and subject matter which, I have been claiming, make dramatic excitements in some measure unavoidable. The "impure, rebellious clay" ("The Incarnation, and Passion") will necessarily rebel and, by equally inescapable necessity, be brought to correction through divine love.[25]

All of these poems, despite their adherence to Reformation formula, would seem to be more intimately revealing of the poet's personal experience and attitudes than the allegorical and abstracted "Regeneration." They expose a variety of selves—all within the range exhibited by Augustine in the *Confessions* and conforming in essentials to the requirements of Lutheran and Calvinist theology, though certainly not less personally urgent and moving for their tendency to fall into established roles. "Anguish," for example, is a poem of passionate supplication and self-surrender in which an Augustinian role

25. See Garner's valuable discussion of the poem headed "Rom. Cap. 8, ver. 19" ("And do they so"), in *Henry Vaughan*, pp. 90–110, which argues against hermetic interpretation and sets the poem's plea for grace against the necessary background of seventeenth-century Augustinian conceptions.

for the self is imagined by Vaughan with unquestionable
personal authenticity.

> My God and King! to thee
> I bow my knee,
> I bow my troubled soul, and greet
> With my foul heart thy holy feet.
> Cast it, or tread it! It shall do
> Even what thou wilt, and praise thee too.
>
> My God, could I weep blood,
> Gladly I would;
> Or if thou wilt give me that Art,
> Which through the eyes pours out the hart,
> I will exhaust it all, and make
> My self all tears, a weeping lake.
>
> O! 'tis an easie thing
> To write and sing;
> But to write true, unfeigned verse
> Is very hard! O God, disperse
> These weights, and give my spirit leave
> To act as well as to conceive!
>
> O my God, hear my cry;
> Or let me dye!

The Augustinian self is, of course, not always surrender-
ing, and even when aiming at obedience and abnegation,
it cannot certainly determine to give up its resistance to
God. The middle stanzas of Vaughan's second poem entitled "Begging" describe the defiance of the "Love-sick
heart"—evidently sick with the misdirected love of Augustine's earthly city—and locates such defiance in a broken
and pitiable humanity.[26]

26. This is not, to be sure, the meaning of "love-sick" in the poem
of that title, nor in "Cock-crowing."

O do not thou do as I did,
Do not despise a Love-sick heart!
What though some clouds defiance bid
Thy Sun must shine in every part.

Though I have spoil'd, O spoil not thou!
Hate not thine own dear gift and token!
Poor birds sing best, and prettiest show,
When their nest is faln and broken.

A sense of humanity fallen and broken emerges more strongly in the second part of *Silex Scintillans* than in the first. There are more tears, more melting expressions of dependency and more insistent pleas for mercy.[27] The themes of weakness in the later poems probably have some connection with Vaughan's evidently increasing problems of health: the second "Begging" alludes to physical illness while pleading for spiritual health—"And if thou wilt not give me ease / from sicknesse, give my spirit health!" In the theology of the poems, however, all that has changed is the outward form of unregeneracy—from (in general) the active recalcitrance imagined in "The Law, and the Gospel"—"since man is a very brute / And after all thy Acts of grace doth kick"—to metaphors of helplessness. In terms of Reformation theology, both are, of course, varieties of human *miseria* which call for action by divine grace. In fact, in both parts of *Silex Scintillans* Vaughan shows extraordinary inventiveness in his metaphors for the unblessed life. In "The Retreat" of Part I, he is helpless rather than rebellious in the famous metaphor of drunkenness: "But (ah!) my soul with too much stay / Is drunk, and staggers in the way."

27. This difference between Part I and Part II of *Silex Scintillans* is perspicaciously described in the unpublished dissertation (Toronto, 1964) by James A. Carscallen, "The Natural World in Vaughan and Marvell," pp. 119–24.

In other poems, the soul without God is dark, dead,
asleep, drowned, a field choked with tares. One poem
alone ("Dressing") describes a soul frozen, empty, confused, soiled, rusty, and locked up. But the unblessed life
is of course not Vaughan's whole subject and is, indeed,
merely a necessary misery on the way to blessedness. Grace
and miracle and transformation are the end in view:

> O come and rend,
> Or bow the heavens! Lord bow them and descend,
> And at thy presence make these mountains flow,
> These mountains of cold Ice in me! Thou art
> Refining fire, O then refine my heart,
> My foul, foul heart! Thou art immortall heat,
> Heat motion gives; Then warm it till it beat,
> So beat for thee, till thou in mercy hear,
> So hear that thou must open: open to
> A sinfull wretch, A wretch that caus'd thy woe,
> Thy woe, who caus'd his weal; so far his weal
> That thou forgott'st thine own, for thou didst seal
> Mine with thy blood, thy blood which makes thee
>   mine,
> Mine ever, ever; And me ever thine.
>   ["Love-sick"]

Vaughan's imagining in such a passage is, of course,
radically Augustinian. Indeed, the words are very near
those with which Augustine describes his own experience
of grace and the misery upon which grace acts:

> Thou calledst, and shoutedst, and burstest my deaf-
> ness. Thou flashedst, shonest, and scatteredst my
> blindness. Thou breathedst odours, and I drew in
> breath and panted for Thee. . . . When I shall with
> my whole self cleave to Thee, I shall nowhere have
> sorrow; or labour; and my life shall wholly live, as

wholly full of Thee. But now since whom Thou fillest, Thou liftest up, because I am not full of Thee I am a burden to myself. Lamentable joys strive with joyous sorrows: and on which side is the victory, I know not. Woe is me! Lord, have pity on me. . . . Woe is me! lo! I hide not my wounds; Thou art the Physician, I the sick; Thou merciful, I miserable.[28]

28. *Confessions,* trans. E. B. Pusey, Everyman's Library (London, n.d.), pp. 227–28.

6   *Paradise Lost*

The qualities that distinguish Milton from the metaphysicals have received a great deal of attention in modern criticism, which early, with Eliot and Pound and
Leavis, fixed on Milton's alleged faults as a means of
promoting Donne and more recently appears inclined to
give judgment against Donne while promoting Milton.
There has been some foolishness in this, and the impression has been given that Milton and the metaphysicals
inhabited wholly disjunct poetic worlds, and that the
English seventeenth century was much more heterogeneous in its ideas than in fact it was. To restore the balance
it is not necessary to suppress real differences: the colloquial vitality valued in the metaphysicals, for example,
is obviously not a quality aimed at by Milton, whose language reflects other purposes; the metaphysicals' peculiar
combinations of homely and esoteric imagery goes another
way from Milton's simple sensuousness and mythological
allusion; and there is little in Milton that can be called
wit.

But there is every possibility, despite these differences, that Milton can be found as complete an Augustinian in poetry as Donne and the other poets of this study. Indeed, a thesis which appears to have some novelty as applied to them may look embarrassingly easy as applied to a poet who so decidedly proclaims himself of the Reformation. However, the formal characteristics of Reformation poetry which concern us—the structural use of the God-Man dualism and reconciliation by grace—have not been fully uncovered in Milton. Dualism of a kind has, of course, been noticed in *Paradise Lost.* In fact, the most familiar complaint about the poem, implicit in critical comment since Blake declared that Milton was "of the devil's party without knowing it," is that it seems to go two ways. It is radically ambivalent, we have been told, reflecting Milton's inability to make his peace with the doctrine he had committed himself to, or to put the full resources of his art in the service of his message—giving attractiveness to what it required to be attractive and unattractiveness to what it required to be unattractive. "Reader after reader testifies," as J. B. Broadbent has said, "to a split, chasm, dichotomy in the poem between ethic and aesthetic, process and sentiment." The elements divided by the chasm have been variously identified. Broadbent, for example, would have it that they are related to strongly opposed impulses in Milton's creative personality, a dipolarity, "at the north heroic (indeed megalomaniac and paranoiac) ambition to pursue things unattempted yet, to comprehend world and chaos, to write something for aftertimes they would not willingly let die; at the south grave acceptance of the recalcitrant data of human existence."[1] Tillyard has gained wide attention for the view that the poles which draw the poem

---

1. *Some Graver Subject* (London, 1960), p. 287.

apart are the contradictions of Milton's conscious and unconscious meanings.[2]

There is usefulness in the "duality" approach to *Paradise Lost,* though one can feel regret at the way these views come across—that the poem should be so meanly accounted for. And it is clear that these dualities are not those which preoccupy the metaphysical poets— the main difference, of course, being that their dualities are those of a reasoned and understood response to the nature of the universe and the problems of man's position in it, whereas the dualities that his critics have found in Milton are merely those of a divided personality and a confused intention. He is not, they tend to say, rendering complexly something that has been complexly appre- hended, but only putting down for all to see what he was unable to see himself—a mere record of his infirmity. But surely it is error to suggest that Milton was the victim, in *Paradise Lost,* of impulses which he did not understand, or that the poem has the characteristics, either the weaknesses or the strengths, of "unconscious art." The vindication of his artistry then is an additional motive for claiming that Milton's dualities are those con- veyed in, if not originally born of, Reformation theology, and now, I trust, shown to be present in other poets of the period.

I shall maintain that *Paradise Lost* contains two "great arguments" rather than one, that each of these takes the form of a coherent set of propositions, and that the op- position between them is not accidental but fully in- tended and constitutes in itself one of the planned *meanings* of the work. The opposition is implicit in the invocation of Book I which hints at two perspectives— the basis of the two arguments—in the first three lines.

2. E. M. W. Tillyard, *Milton,* 2d ed. (London, 1949).

The heavenly muse is invited to assist the poet in his
attempt to treat

> Of Man's First Disobedience, and the Fruit
> Of that Forbidden Tree, whose mortal taste,
> Brought Death into the World, and all our woe . . .[3]

It deserves attention that there is a single referent for
"Man" in the first line and "our" in the third—both
referring, of course, to the human race. Obviously, what
signals dualism in the two references is that one is in
the third person and the other in the first: *Man's* disobedience, *our* woe. In the one place man is being viewed
from the outside, in the other place from the inside; we
move from a "he" to an "us" perspective. And the percep-
tions attached to these linguistic indicators change accordingly. Viewed from the outside the importance of what
happens in the poem is that man disobeys. Viewed from
the inside, what is important is the consequence of his
disobedience—the dreadfulness of human history in the
lump, as seen in the last books of the poem, and the
tragedy of the individual human life—"all our woe."
The terms "inside" and "outside" are useful but perhaps
tantalize more than they satisfy. The inside view, as we
have seen, is the human view. The outside view is, of
course, God's. The two are maintained consistently in
the poem, each reflecting independently upon the action,
and neither having a measurable effect upon the other.
The failure of connection between them is, in fact, both
an event *in* the poem and a cause for it. It is because the
human perspective continues (in us as in Adam) to exclude the divine, because man continues baffled by the
disparity between desire and event, between what ought

3. The edition of *Paradise Lost* cited throughout is *Complete
Poems and Major Prose,* ed. Merritt Y. Hughes (New York, 1957).

to be (or apparently ought to be) and what is in God's
creation, that it is necessary to "justify the ways of God
to men." (For, as the angel Uriel asks in another connection, "What created mind can comprehend?") The two
perspectives miss congruity so far that God's justice can
seem to man to be unjust, a contradiction which more
vividly than any other illuminates the "chasm" between
the human and divine which only grace can bridge.

The chasm opens over the question of the guilt of the
fall—which God sees from an exclusive, divine point of
view. Even in anticipation of the fall he appears angry,
foretelling that

> Man will heark'n to [Satan's] glozing lies,
> And easily transgress the sole Command,
> Sole pledge of his obedience: So will fall
> Hee and his faithless Progeny: whose fault?
> Whose but his own? Ingrate, he had of mee
> All he could have; I made him just and right,
> Sufficient to have stood, though free to fall.
>
> [III, 93–99]

> . . . they themselves decreed
> Thir own revolt, not I . . .
>
> [III, 116–17]

> They trespass, Authors to themselves in all
>
> .   .   .   .
>
> . . . they themselves ordain'd thir fall
>
> [III, 122–28]

The son moderates this harshness, but in doing so adds
to the divine case against man the charge of folly (III,
144–66). Satan's fraud and man's own "folly" lead to
the act of disobedience. God's next speech announces the
theme of man's pride and superhuman aspiration and
passes the death sentence.

> . . . Man disobeying,
> Disloyal, breaks his fealty, and sins
> Against the high Supremacy of Heav'n,
> Affecting God-head, and so losing all,
> To expiate his Treason hath naught left,
> But to destruction sacred and devote,
> He with his whole posterity must die,
> Die hee or Justice must . . .
>
> [III, 203–10]

To be sure, God immediately proposes a way out—"the rigid satisfaction, death for death," of Christ's sacrifice, but it is a way out that does nothing to diminish human guilt. It is "Man's mortal crime"—the heinousness of which in the heavenly perspective only makes plainer God's infinite mercy. The angelic chorus evidently sets a right value on this in their song of praise:

> Father of Mercy and Grace, thou didst not doom
> So strictly, but much more to pity incline:
>
> . . . .
>
> . . . O unexampl'd love,
> Love nowhere to be found less than Divine!
>
> [III, 401–11]

This is the full range of God's opinions regarding man's position and his own at the fall. He himself has been generous in the gift of freedom before the fall and in offering grace and mercy afterwards. Man's folly, ingratitude, aspiration to godhead and misplaced loyalty stand in vivid contrast. The view is stated repeatedly as the poem offers opportunity for God, Raphael, Michael, and—willy-nilly—Satan to justify the ways of God. Raphael, sent according to the Argument of Book V to "admonish [Adam] of his obedience, of his free estate, of his enemy near at hand, who he is and why his enemy," devotes most

of his conversation to a parable-history which justifies
God's demeanor toward another miscreant and, of course,
by extension, to Adam and Eve. In God's view, God
asks little enough and provides what is necessary to ful-
fill his conditions:

> . . . Son of Heav'n and Earth, [says Raphael]
> Attend: That thou art happy, owe to God;
> That thou continu'st such, owe to thyself,
> That is, to thy obedience; therein stand.
>
> .   .   .   .
>
> God made thee perfet, not immutable;
> And good he made thee, but to persevere
> He left it in thy power, ordain'd thy will
> By nature free, not overrul'd by Fate
> Inextricable, or strict necessity.
>
> [V, 519–43]

Three books later, after concluding some anxious counsel
to Adam on the human duty to subordinate passion to
reason and on the necessity for Adam to assert himself
as Eve's rational superior, Raphael takes his leave still
insisting that "to stand or fall / Free in thine own arbitra-
ment it lies" (VIII, 640–41).

God's case is clear. Man's rational and moral compet-
ence established, his failure to obey is aggressive wrong-
doing, and stern punishment is just. God in Book X, after
the fall, is consistent with himself in Book III: nothing
has changed but his tenses.

> I told ye then he should prevail and speed
> On his bad Errand, Man should be seduc't
>
> .   .   .   .
>
> . . . no Decree of mine
> Concurring to necessitate his Fall,
> Or touch with lightest moment of impulse

His free Will, to her own inclining left
In even scale. But fall'n he is, and now
What rests, but that the mortal sentence pass
On his transgression . . .

. . . .

Justice shall not return as bounty scorn'd.

[X, 40–54]

The first champion of the human perspective in the poem is not Adam but Satan, who in every circumstance but one—the impossibility of his redemption—duplicates the spiritual characteristics and situation of sinful man. He is the first author of division from God, which man persistently renews, the arch-foe, "th' Antagonist of Heav'n" who seems alone in that role because the roles of Adam and Eve—limited primarily to the uses of Milton's providence theme—allow no real scope for the depiction of the outrageousness of human sin as conscious, willful antagonism to the will of God and rejection of his love. Unlike that of their descendants, their own sin does not, so far as the poem shows us, cut off absolutely their communion with heaven, though Milton's tragic notes convey that Heaven's response will include "distance and distaste." And however complete and reprehensible their act of sin, blamable as "foul distrust and breach disloyal . . . revolt and disobedience," it seems clear that Milton did not design them for rebellion. Indeed, beginning as they do in innocence, they require to be seduced into sin, making their revolt and disobedience seem somewhat abstract.

Satan's revolt, on the other hand, is not abstract, but vividly dramatized and immediate, and his attitudes of opposition and self-regard correspond in essentials to Protestant conceptions of sin. Indeed, the vigor of the characterization of Satan, which has seduced some un-theological readers of the poem to think him its hero, is largely a function of the *activeness* of sin and self, in the Augustinian conception, in rejecting God—whose role in this separation is to suffer the loss of his creature almost passively. The sinful creature acts, in sin, while God is simply acted against (until the process and the roles are reversed in reconciliation, and God becomes active in unifying what sin has made separate).

Satan's first speech in the poem is full of hyperactive "heroics" with unconscious theological double meanings which collect layer on layer to define essential sin—the human self's resistance to God's will. Milton reminds us frequently that the human argument or human perspective in his poem is a wrong one, a point made strongly here by lodging its distortions in the mind of Satan, who is all the more potent a symbol for the fact that in his infatuated pushing of the claims of self he seems to have become insensitized to the primary meanings of his words. He speaks in self-celebration of his "unconquerable Will," naming the errant faculty condemned by Augustine and all his heirs, and he pledges "study of revenge, immortal hate / And courage never to submit or yield" (I, 107–08). But immortal hate is, of course, intolerable from the standpoint of either psychology or religion, and "never to submit" to God is never to enjoy blessedness, which *is* submission—"to observe / Immutably his sovran will, the end / Of what we are" (VII, 78–80). Satan would have it that not to submit is "not to be overcome," but being overcome by God, in the theology Milton knew best, is the only real triumph of the soul; the alternative being the captivity of the self which is the soul's destruction.

C. S. Lewis and others have found Satan's attitudes in this speech comically foolish, which undoubtedly they are, but the comedy of Satan's defiance includes all of the essential materials of the spiritual tragedy of man. It is the fundamental human error, and not merely Satanic, to scorn to "bow and sue for grace / With suppliant knee and deify [God's] power." The deification of God is merely the recognition of his godhood, a necessary operation of *faith,* the only spiritual qualification allowed man in Reformation theology (echoed variously by Milton; see, e.g., *De Doctrina Christiana* I, iv, where he cites St. Paul: "thou standeth by faith," Rom. 11:7). To bow and sue for grace is "ignominy," as Satan puts it, only in the perspective of a deluded self-interest unable to recognize the soul's true glory and in full flight from its appointed good.[4]

That deluded, human perspective finds matter for pride in "strife not inglorious" against the Almighty which is in fact contradictory to every acceptable meaning of glory; it takes the perfect harmony of heaven, where God's will is unopposed, for a "Tyranny" and declares "eternal war Irreconcilable [again Satan's unwitting theological precision] to our grand Foe." It is a perspective which clings to conventions of status and personal autonomy and identity: "What matter where, if I be still the same, / And what I should be . . ." (I, 256–57); and it falls into egocentric confusions of the grounds for hope and fear. That the "mind and spirit remains invincible" to the batterings of God is a catastrophe, not a victory; "to be weak is miserable" is an opinion which overlooks the momentous certainty that weakness in contention with God is a condition of happiness. Satan is simply making man's mistakes. On the other hand, he has a clarity about his chosen direction that Milton would have had to deny to a merely human spokesman. To

4. Cf. Calvin: "In the Divine view . . . what is reputed glory is real ignominy" (*Institutes of the Christian Religion*, trans. John Allen, 7th ed. [Philadelphia, 1945], 3.xii.4).

"resist" God and do that which is "contrary to his high will" is to do that which Satan recognizes as essential evil and embraces under that name. The opposition of sinful man to God is the same evil, but it is characteristically "human" for man to deceive himself with the explanation that he has chosen not evil, but an alternative good (although, when fallen, Adam will know better, seeing himself as "To Satan only like . . ."). Here, as elsewhere by different routes, Satan leads us to right theological identifications.

His egocentricity, which has drawn comment from many readers, is undoubtedly his main theologically significant characteristic. It is sometimes hectic and uncontrolled, as when he is surprised by Gabriel's guard and insists shrilly on being recognized for the great person he is. This contrasts in mood, though not in theological implication, with the cool genius of self-assertion shown in his manipulation of the infernal debate to assure that "none shall partake" with him in the glory of his adventure out of hell. But whatever the mood of his self-devotion there is no mistaking that self-devotion is in fact Satan's root passion. He exhibits exactly that "love of self even to contempt of God" which Augustine condemns in the *City of God* and which recurs in Reformation theology as the opposite of Christian liberty. It is not liberating, as we know, for Satan, whose plight is described to him by Abdiel: "Thyself not free, but to thyself enthrall'd." Satan's self-estimate is at least as bleak—"myself am Hell." Indeed, the hell of self is a theme sounded consistently with Satan's appearances in the poem, giving emphasis to the absoluteness of opposition between the self-on-its-own and heaven. It is surely this that is intended (with Satan again unwitting) in the famous boast in Book I, where Satan declares his readiness to accept hell and asserts the supremacy of mind over accidents of location:

> The mind is its own place, and in itself
> Can make a Heav'n of Hell, a Hell of Heav'n.[5]
>
> [I. 254–55]

Some labor and ingenuity have been spent to find the medieval sources of Satan's "heresy" in thus reducing heaven and hell to mere subjective states. The investigation is an interesting one, but neglects a setting of ideas which Milton evidently considered vital in favor of a minor theological curiosity. It would seem more serviceable in the interpretation of the poem as a whole to read the passage in the light of the "great divorce" of man and God which preoccupied Reformation theology. In that light, explication need not be elaborate: Satan is describing the perversion of mind and will that rejects God for the love of self. Insofar as that rejection constitutes essential evil it can be said to make a "hell," and indeed in Reformation opinion, it put the soul at hell's distance from heaven; that is, brought about total separation. But Satan's account of the act of sin is accurate in both halves, for there is a complementary sense in which sin makes a "heaven" by misdevotion; the mind closing upon itself and giving self the love that belongs to God produces a corrupt parody of right devotion (as Satan's hell parodies God's heaven.) Hell is, in fact, Satan's alternative heaven, preferred for the scope it gives to self.

> Here we may reign secure, and in my choice
> To reign is worth ambition though in Hell:
> Better to reign in Hell, than serve in Heav'n
>
> [I, 261–63]

Heaven requires service, or the submission of self, which is fully free in hell, the self's autonomous empire.

5. There is a valuable discussion of these lines and of the "Satanic symbol" in Roland M. Frye's *God, Man and Satan* (Princeton, 1960), pp. 21–41.

For the Reformation, as we have seen, the theological expression of self-regard was the claim of human merit, that superstition of natural reason upheld by Rome which encouraged man to believe that he could gain admittance to heaven by the offer of his righteousness to God. Unfallen Adam knows better than this, seeing correctly that man has "nothing merited" from God, "nor can perform aught whereof hee hath need" (IV, 418–19). Satan's speeches, however, echo and reecho with this error of human nature and Rome; and Milton has given him, here also, a language designed to play tc Reformation responses.

In the first words of self-appraisal with which he breaks the horrid silence of the burning lake, he tells of the continuing potency of his "fixt mind and high disdain, from sense of injured merit" and is quick to apply this conceit of inherent worth and power to the problem of recovering heaven:

> For who can yet believe, though after loss,
> That all these puissant Legions, whose exile
> Hath emptied Heav'n, shall fail to re-ascend
> Self-rais'd, and repossess thir native seat?
>
> [I, 631–34]

Enthroned at the opening of Book II—"by merit rais'd to that bad eminence"—he resumes encouraging his followers to hope to regain heaven by their own effort and excellence. Celestial Virtues will rise again, fearless and self-trusting; he himself will continue to lead as in the past, in part on the basis of what "hath been achiev'd of merit." It seems clear that if Satan "insatiate to pursue vain war with heaven" and bent on doing "the contrary of his high will," symbolizes the action of the human self in willful rebellion, then Satan mouthing merit symbolizes the equally erroneous exertions of the self in

spiritual ambition: "Great things resolv'd, which from
the lowest deep / Will once more lift us up" (II, 392–93).
Great resolves, flexings of the will, are at best irrelevant
according to Reformation arguments, and the way to rise
is shown us in the Son, whose "Manhood" will be exalted
by humiliation (III, 313–14) and whose merit alone has
redemptive virtue. We learn of it, as he does, from the
Father:

> . . . thy merit
> Imputed shall absolve them who renounce
> Thir own both righteous and unrighteous deeds,
> And live in thee transplanted, and from thee
> Receive new life. . . .
>
> [III, 290–94]

Such renunciations are, of course, not made by self-
captived, unregenerate man, nor by Satan, his magnific
representative in the poem; self will insist on its achieve-
ments.

Satan's usefulness as a symbol for a theologically defined condition of man does not detract from his authority and power as the embodiment of evil at the supernatural level. One does not intend to challenge the view
that Milton "believed in the devil" or to imply that the
theology of the Augustinian revival had not "accepted
the theory of the Angels' rebellion in heaven as a fact."[6]
Doubtless the Satan-man parallelism was in part forced
on Milton by the fact that he had only the one, essentially
Augustinian, concept of evil. Willful and self-infatuated
rebellion against the will of God is a single, though comprehensive, sin, irrespective of the identity of the rebel,
and a Satan wholly different from sinful man was not to
be imagined in Milton's theology. On the evidence just

6. C. A. Patrides, *Milton and the Christian Tradition* (Oxford,
1966), p. 91.

considered, however, it seems clear that Milton worked out the parallelism with deliberateness and in detail, and that he relied on Satan to illustrate primary arguments concerning the nature of human sin. For Satan shares even our confusion and declares a need as clear as ours of a poem which will justify God's ways and explain the conundrum of "His wrath which he calls Justice" (II, 732).

The human argument is raised in a different form in Adam and Eve, though inevitably reflecting the same confusion, and implying, at least, a similar self-justification and complaint against God, whose justice seems overexacting and provision for his creatures inadequate. Adam, in momentary darkness after the Fall, finds God's justice "inexplicable" and his "terms too hard." Empson is making, rather than describing, a version of this argument when he denounces Milton's God for "mean-mindedness" and "malignity."[7] (The dialectic of the poem of Augustinian opposites, as we have seen in other examples, may exploit the "human" sympathies of the reader, tempting him into participation in unregenerate attitudes for the sake of sharp correction. Empson simply fails to take correction.)[8] Milton allows Adam and Eve no such scope and energy of complaint; indeed, they speak sometimes from God's perspective. The elements of the human case against God emerge, however, as much in their circumstances as in what they say, and are evidently intended to contrast with the truth about God as revealed in God's own statements about himself and his purposes, in the discourses of Raphael, in the action described in the poem and in Milton's comments on the action.

7. William Empson, *Milton's God*, rev. ed. (London, 1965).

8. Milton's techniques of teaching through participation are more fully discussed in Stanley Fish, *Surprised by Sin: The Reader in Paradise Lost* (New York, 1967); see especially pp. 1–56.

What Adam and Eve are allowed, chiefly, is a somewhat
wavering challenge to God's insistence, as expressed by
Raphael, that "God made man perfect," therefore adequately guarded against temptation and justly punished
when he falls. According to the divine perspective, Adam
should "Accuse not Nature, for she hath done her part" (a
view also adopted by Adam in his discourse to Eve of
reason and will, early in Book IX). [9] Yet the poem seems
to give evidence that Man might have been started with
more complete equipment, that human accusation has
some point. Adam's first words on earth include a declaration that whereas in God "is no deficience found; not so
is Man." The deficiency comes fully into view in Book
VIII, in Adam's account of his own creation and Eve's
and in Raphael's warning to Adam concerning the sub-
versive forces in his own nature. (The point is still being
repeated in Book XII, when Michael observes in fallen
man that "upstart Passions may catch the Government
from Reason.") Eve's nature is even less well fortified and
she is so extremely attractive in her frailty that she seems
designed to bring on catastrophe. She reduces Adam, even
in innocence, almost to helplessness. The rest of the creation, he tells Raphael, he can enjoy soberly and ration-
ally. Eve is another matter. "Here," he says,

9. The easy plausibility of a human case against God is a crux
for Calvin also, who makes what defense he can against "those who
dare to charge God with their corruptions." We are indeed *naturally*
corrupt, but not made so by God. "Our perdition . . . proceeds from
the sinfulness of our flesh, not from God, it being only a consequence
of our degenerating from our primitive condition. And let no one
murmur that God might have made a better provision for our
safety. . . . Wherefore let us remember that our ruin must be imputed to the corruption of our nature that we may not bring an
accusation against God himself, the author of Nature" *(Institutes,*
2.i.10).

> ... transported I behold,
> Transported touch; here passion first I felt,
> Commotion strange ...
>
> [VIII, 528–30]

The disturbance raises for Adam the question whether
he possesses a whole and adequate human constitution.

> Or Nature fail'd in mee, and left some part
> Not proof enough such Object to sustain,
> Or from my side subducting, took perhaps
> More than enough ...
>
> [VIII, 534–37]

His response to his fellow creature staggers him in its
excessiveness, which he recognizes but cannot control.

> ... when I approach
> Her loveliness, so absolute she seems
> And in herself complete, so well to know
> Her own, that what she wills to do or say,
> Seems wisest, virtuousest, discreetest, best;
> All higher knowledge in her presence falls
> Degraded, Wisdom in discourse with her
> Loses, discount'nanc't, and like folly shows;
> Authority and Reason on her wait,
> As one intended first, not after made
> Occasionally ...
>
> [VIII, 546–56]

One may have difficulty accepting the notion that when
Adam falls it is through being overcome by "femal
charm" as Milton insists (in neglect, according to a common opinion, of the story he has told), but it is clear that
Eve has sufficient resources of femaleness and charm to
bring about such a result, if Adam required to be moved
by them.

Eve has been faulted by Tillyard for "triviality of mind," a phrase which seems to fit, especially in those crucial passages where she allows Satan to make headway by flattering her into believing herself a unique human marvel—"sovran mistress" and "sole wonder" of creatures. Adam is not unfair, later, in reproaching her with "pride and wandering vanity." But it seems unhelpable, given the qualities with which God has endowed the human mind. Adam observes that

> . . . apt the Mind or Fancy is to rove
> Uncheckt, and of her roving is no end;
> Till, warn'd, or by experience taught, she learn.
>
> [VIII, 188–90]

The limits of curiosity are learned by catastrophic experience in Paradise, as, apparently, they must be. But the mind is really not dependable, as Adam warns Eve when she suggests that they divide their labors.

> . . . Reason not impossibly may meet
> Some specious object by the Foe suborn'd
> And fall into deception unaware.
>
> [IX, 360–62]

Eve has already argued tellingly for the necessity of divine help to sustain them in their weakness.

> And what is Faith, Love, Virtue unassay'd
> Alone, without exterior help sustain'd?
> Let us not then suspect our happy State
> Left so imperfet by the Maker wise,
> As not secure to single or combin'd.
> Frail is our happiness, if this be so,
> And *Eden* were no *Eden* thus expos'd.
>
> [IX, 335–41]

But man would seem to be justified by more in his
nature than his innate weaknesses. The heavenly in-
formants are absolute on the point that reason, whatever
its uncertainties, is man's defining quality (corrupted at
the Fall). "Human" and "rational" are synonymous terms,
as appears for example in Raphael's urging Adam to
love Eve only for "What higher in her society thou
find'st / Attractive, human, rational." Both for the purpose then of fulfilling her humanity and of establishing
terms of greater intimacy with heaven, Eve would seem
inevitably to have been attracted to eat the fruit that
promised more reason. It is not mere folly for a creature
whose essential and best constituent is X to seek its improvement in more X—it would seem to be following
a law of its nature. And Eve is not *merely* trivial when
she falls, as we are told she does, with godhead in her
thoughts—though she is of course open to the charge of
pride and spiritual ambition. Moreover, some of Satan's
arguments to her must be allowed to have at least the appearance of plausibility to ordinary reason.

> Shall that be shut to Man, which to the Beast
> Is open? or will God incense his ire
> For such a petty Trespass, and not praise
> Rather your dauntless virtue, whom the pain
> Of Death denounc't, whatever thing Death be,
> Deterr'd not from achieving what might lead
> To happier life, knowledge of Good and Evil;
> Of good, how just? of evil, if what is evil
> Be real, why not known, since easier shunn'd?
> God therefore cannot hurt ye, and be just.
>
> [IX, 691–700]

Satan is echoed in Empson's lively book attacking God.
There appears to be something to the point of view, if we
consider it alone, suppressing God's argument—which
means, however, the suppression of Milton's theology.

The human justification for Adam seems more clear-cut than for Eve, or less ambiguously related to the imperatives of the inconvenient human nature God has given him. He falls, in a word, for fellowship, or, from the other side, through fear of solitude. This is not to set aside the statement in the Argument of Book IX that he falls "through vehemence of love" or the statement later in the book that he is "fondly overcome with femal charm." It is to suppose, however, as some readers seem not to, that Adam's fond regard for Eve is a constant characteristic of their prelapsarian relationship. He is an enthusiastic husband who celebrates his wife in high terms, and his admiration appears to be less vehement rather than more when he takes the apple. His mood is not one of reinvigorated amorous appetite but of "sad dismay . . . submitting to what seemed remediless."

The themes of fellowship and solitude, which supply motives for Adam's action, are major themes in the poem and deserve more attention than they have received. They are introduced with Adam's first speech to his creator, after the naming of the creatures, pair by pair:

> . . . with mee
> I see not who partakes. In solitude
> What happiness . . . ?
>
> [VIII, 364–66]

Adam answers God's teasing response to this with an earnest argument for the necessity of human society and wins his way finally, as God intends him to, with the argument that man is

> In unity defective, which requires
> Collateral love and dearest amity.
>
> [VIII, 425–26]

The creation of Eve is provided for in the next lines, from Adam's own body. Their relationship is symbolized

in this creation: they have more than an association;
they are two-in-one, as Adam's language fully conveys in
the lines which recognize the event:

> . . . I now see
> Bone of my Bone, Flesh of my Flesh, my Self
> Before me; Woman is her Name, of Man
> Extracted; for this cause he shall forgo
> Father and Mother, and to his Wife adhere;
> And they shall be one Flesh, one Heart, one Soul.
>
> [VIII, 494–99]

Like Satan, Adam says somewhat better than he knows:
Eve *is* flesh of his flesh, himself—and the love of woman,
for which, in effect, he abandons God, has a relation to
the love of self. (As St. Paul can be invoked to show: "He
that loveth his wife loveth himself" Eph. 5:29.) Adam's
statement of his human feelings is disarming, especially
in its hint of duty—forgo and adhere—but it announces
the birth of a perspective, simultaneous with the birth
of man, in which human obligations are primary. At the
fall, the language is repeated.[10]

---

10. Milton's editors have commonly noted the allusion to Genesis
2:22–24 ("This is now bone of my bones, and flesh of my flesh: she
shall be called Woman, because she was taken out of Man"), which
is repeated in Matthew 19:4–6 and Mark 10:6–8. Milton is at least
as likely to be echoing Ephesians 5:30, however, where the same
metaphors of marriage are used to describe the relation of the Lord
to his church: "for we are members of his body, of his flesh, and of
his bones." Calvin draws on this passage in describing the life of the
renewed soul in God, who "by the breath of his power . . . inspires
us with Divine life, so that we are not now actuated from ourselves,
but directed by his agency and influence; so that if there be any
good in us, it is the fruit of his grace . . . that sacred marriage, by
which we are made flesh of his flesh and bone of his bone, and
therefore one with him" *(Institutes,* 3.i.3). Adam, as has been often
remarked, confuses his earthly with his heavenly obligation.

> ... no no, I feel
> The Link of Nature draw me: Flesh of Flesh,
> Bone of my Bone thou art, and from thy State
> Mine never shall be parted, bliss or woe.
>
> [IX, 913–16]

The attitude could not be more strongly insisted upon in the multiple repetitions in the poem of the ideas of mutual identity and complex unity and the intensifying literal force of such terms as "bond of Nature," "union," "one." A last example:

> ... I with thee have fixt my Lot,
> Certain to undergo like doom; if Death
> Consort with thee, Death is to mee as Life;
> So forcible within my heart I feel
> The Bond of Nature draw me to my own,
> My own in thee, for what thou art is mine;
> Our State cannot be sever'd; we are one,
> One Flesh; to love thee were to lose myself.
>   So *Adam*, and thus *Eve* to him repli'd.
> O glorious trial of exceeding Love,
> Illustrious evidence, example high!
> Ingaging me to emulate, but short
> Of thy perfection, how shall I attain,
> *Adam*, from whose dear side I boast me sprung,
> And gladly of our Union hear thee speak,
> One Heart, one Soul in both; whereof good proof
> This day affords, declaring thee resolv'd,
> Rather than Death or aught than Death more dread
> Shall separate us, linkt in Love so dear
> To undergo with mee one Guilt, one Crime.
>
> [IX, 952–71]

It has been said of Donne that, "For us today, Donne's imagination seems obsessed with the problem of unity;

the sense in which the lovers become one—the sense in which the soul is united to God."[11] Milton's obsession seems as great, and, if the thesis of this study is correct, both should be seen as stemming from a dominant and persistent habit of Reformation thought. The ideas of separation and union are capable of various applications, however, even within a limited theological context, and their use in the passage just quoted appears designed to show that it is not only necessary and inevitable but, in the human perspective, meritorious that Adam should resist return to the "defects of loneliness" by following Eve into sin.

The themes of fellowship and solitude are obviously important in the account of the fall. It may be noted, however, that the usefulness of these themes in *Paradise Lost* is not exhausted in their function of illuminating causes. They appear also as conditions—significantly varied conditions—wherever the poet attempts to give a character to happiness or misery, reward or punishment, guilt or innocence. Perfect blessedness is perfect union—the condition which will obtain after the final judgment when man's fall will have proven to be fortunate after all, and God will cease to rule over the creation as something distinct from himself, but will be simply "All in All." It is a condition anticipated in the life of Eden where "the fair couple linked in happy nuptial league" is at one with a nature which provides entertainment by all the beasts of the earth—"tame and friendly then, though since grown wild"; and it is symbolized most arrestingly in the account of the intercourse of angels—"total they mix."

11. Cleanth Brooks, *The Well-Wrought Urn* (New York, 1947), p. 19.

The fall produces rupture. In Adam and Eve the words "mixt with Love / And sweet compliance, which declare unfeign'd / Union of Mind" (VIII, 602–04), change to angry recriminations. Adam is described as "estranged in look and style" and declares his wish that he might "in solitude live savage." In providing themselves with clothing they provide a physical symbol of estrangement. But they are estranged from God as well as each other, a consequence which follows immediately upon the first taste of the fruit. Eve hopes that she may have escaped detection because heaven, with which connections had been intimate, now seems "high—high and remote"; moreover the great "Forbidder" and his angels, now distrusted as "spies," may have been busy with other things. God has said in Book V that "him who disobeys Mee disobeys, breaks union," and now alienation is mutual and complete:

> No more of talk where God or Angel Guest
> With Man, as with his Friend, familiar us'd
> To sit indulgent . . .
>
> [IX, 1–3]

In short, the conditions of existence begin to be established which account for the double perspective in the poem.

The return of man to his "single imperfection" in the fallen world is perhaps most vividly symbolized in the Tower of Babel episode in Book XII. Nimrod—"one of proud, ambitious heart," and thus a reenactor of Satan's sin and, in perhaps more ways than I have allowed, of Adam and Eve's—attempts with bricks cemented by excrescent matter of Hell "to build / a City and Tow'r, whose top may reach to Heav'n"—a clear enough parallel to Eve's appetite for godhood. The end of this

adventure is the derisive laughter of God at human over-
weeningness and the sundering of man from man by
setting

> Upon thir Tongues a various Spirit to rase
> Quite out thir Native Language, and instead
> To sow a jangling noise of words unknown;
>
> [XII, 53–55]

Communication is at an end as a "hideous gabble rises
loud among the Builders."

What pride, ambition, and self-assertion put apart,
however, love can put back together. Thus God and man
merge through divine love in the person of Christ—in
whom "God with Man unites" and who counteracts
the catastrophe of Babel by sending out his apostles to
evangelize the nations, giving them the "wondrous gift
. . . to speak all tongues." And the blessedness of the
paradise within is achieved by Man's suppression of self
in social love. But in the fallen world, this social love is
rare and lacking in social rewards. Virtue and righteousness and love become solitary, and the postlapsarian
paradise within exists in isolation as complete as Satan's
prelapsarian hell within. And just as Satan is assailed by
the powers of Goodness, the isolated good are assailed
by the powers of evil. The poet of the invocation in
Book VII sees his own situation thus, writing in "evil
days" among evil people, and apprehensive of injury
from "the race of that wild Rout that tore the Thracian
Bard." Enoch is the "only righteous in a world perverse."
Moses is "the one just man alive" and is despised. The
climax of the sequence occurs, of course, with Christ who
comes with greatest love to meet the greatest scorn—"to a
reproachful life and a cursed death." The cost of fellowship with God in a world grown evil is isolation from
men.

It is because the world is evil, presumably, and men are remote from God that they require to have the ways of God justified to them—or this at least is how it appears in the divine perspective, which Milton clearly means to throw his own authority behind in the end. Fellowship with God requires faith, which requires abandonment of the human challenge to the nature of things. Samson's chorus will say, "All is best though oft we doubt" and intend application to the world described by Michael as "to good malignant, to bad men benign." To know this and to be "simply meek" is the "sum of wisdom."

We want to protest, of course; *Paradise Lost* had not seemed to be going this way, and there seems to be no excuse for the scuttling of the human perspective. But Milton has chosen for God before this, as his justifying purpose has committed him to do, and has been calling human error by its worst names at a good many points in the poem: "foul distrust, and breach / Disloyal on the part of Man, revolt / And disobedience" (IX, 6–8). The machinery of reconciliation is operating here in the fashion that should now be familiar to us. Two voices have been heard, or two perspectives exposed; a unity is aimed at, however, and in *Paradise Lost* as in the other poems of our study it is achieved not by an unmanipulated playing out of the dialogue, nor by combination, but by declaring one voice authoritative and silencing the other. Milton *asserts* Eternal Providence.

What perhaps most needs arguing in such a reading of the poem is the notion that it is Providence, God in his reconciling aspect, that is the primary theme of *Paradise Lost* and the ultimate silencer of debate. Milton has been unlucky in some readers—Empson is a recent example—who have seen more of divine justice in the poem than divine mercy. God must, of course, denounce sin, and does so with some ferocity, but there is nothing ferocious

in his dealing with man, who, if justice only were to
be served, would be swiftly "adjudg'd to Death and
Hell,"—not redeemed, but "blot[ted] out" (XI, 891). But
Milton insists that God's "mercy first and last shall
brightest shine," and it is worth remarking that while the
Son may appear to have the special function of tempering
justice with mercy, the "anti-Trinitarian" Milton will not
give him sole responsibility for mercy or independent
possession of any divine attribute. The Son is the agent
of the Father ("Father Eternal, thine is to decree, /
Mine both in Heav'n and Earth to do thy will /
supreme"). His mercy is the mercy of the Father, or,
rather, of a single divine impulse. Heaven is the "Mercy-
seat" and designing place of the Reformation's only
miracle, "Immortal love to mortal man." The creation
itself is an act of love by which God intends to "diffuse
his good" and which Milton brackets with significant
symmetry in the middle of his poem with the wrath and
destruction scenes of Book VI. Man is not to be treated
like the rebellious angels, but is to enjoy the benefits of
special favor in a special setting vitalized by God's active
presence; the *grace landscape* which we have glanced at
briefly in the psalms and in Marvell's "Bermudas" is
gigantically generalized, imaging a still more overwhelming divine solicitude, in Milton's account of the creation
of nature.

> And God created the great Whales, and each
> Soul living, each that crept, which plenteously
> The waters generated by thir kinds,
> And every Bird of wing after his kind;
> And saw that it was good, and bless'd them.
>
> [VII, 391–95]

The creation is, in fact, a "reconciling" act, as the Son
departs from heaven with "love immense" to command

"Silence, ye troubl'd waves, and thou Deep, peace." After
the Fall, man can expect, not desertion, but continuing
divine presence "still compassing thee round with goodness and paternal Love. . . . supernal Grace contending
with sinfulness of Man." The atonement is the climactic
episode in this long contention, demonstrating the "ful-
ness . . . of love divine" to man dead in sins and lost,
bestowed by a godhead (not merely the Son) in whom
"Love hath abounded more than Glory abounds" (III,
312). Finally the Creation shall end as it began, in a
triumph of love and reconciliation, and the merging of
God into everything and of everything into God. There
shall be

> New Heav'n and Earth, wherein the just shall dwell
> And after all thir tribulations long
> See golden days, fruitful of golden deeds,
> With Joy and Love triumphing, and fair Truth.
> Then thou thy regal Sceptre shalt lay by,
> For regal Sceptre then no more shall need,
> God shall be All in All.
>
> [III, 334–40]

Appendix: Milton's Arianism and Arminianism

I will seem to have made Milton too much a Calvinist to satisfy some opinions and been too neglectful of his well-known "heresies" for others. The Milton who was "a sect in himself" has not appeared. Nor has the Milton of the permanent Christian center, "Catholic" in the sense of holding conceptions that have been held "always and everywhere by all." I have invoked St. Augustine, not for what he tells us about Milton's hierarchies, but as a main figure in the background of his (implicitly unhierarchic) Reformation dualism. These various departures from what has become familiar method in treating Milton's religion appear justified when we turn to his theological treatise.

I shall pass the question, which has been adequately discussed by others, whether positions developed in the *De Doctrina Christiana* are fully exhibited in *Paradise Lost* and simply try to show, without laboring the obvious, that the *De Doctrina* does support such a reading of the poem as I have suggested and that it is very completely a Reformation document. The *De Doctrina* asks insistently to have its originality respected, and

Milton calls attention repeatedly to his intention to "scrutinize and ascertain for myself," resolving not to "repose on the faith or judgment of others" and declaring himself indifferent whether he should "differ from certain received opinions." Most students of Milton's religion have been overready, I believe, to accept these suggestions of novelty and to neglect the evidence that Milton's theological freedoms are being taken within acknowledged Reformation limits, and are identified by Milton as contributions to a progress begun "since the commencement of the last century, when religion began to be restored from the corruptions of more than thirteen hundred years to something of its original purity."

Milton's Arianism, perhaps his most frequently cited heresy, is a position taken up much more conspicuously in the *De Doctrina* than in *Paradise Lost,* where his account of the relations among the members of the holy Trinity is muted to a quiet (though of course un-Nicene) "subordinationism." Even in the *De Doctrina,* however, Milton does not go head-over-heels into heresy, and when he says that the Son is "not in the highest sense divine," he does not mean that he is less than divine, but that he is "only next in dignity to God."[1] He claims, of course, a scriptural basis for his views on the Trinity, and the right of a Protestant to read scripture for himself. And while he allows that his conception of the Trinity may deviate from common opinion, he considers that he is taking no unlicensed freedoms and sees "no reason why any one who belongs to the same Protestant or Reformed Church, and professes to acknowledge the same rule of faith as myself should take offense" *(Works,* 14:177). Indeed, he was undoubtedly well aware that his antitrinitarianism had been anticipated, often in much more aggressive and absolute forms in a variety of Reformation and pre-

1. *The Works of John Milton,* ed. F. H. Patterson (New York, 1933), 14: 337.

Reformation sources including the Italian reformers, certain humanist critics such as Valla and Ficino, and in the
lively Protestant controversies of Hungary and Poland.
It appeared wherever Anabaptism spread and was a
constant feature of the doctrine of the most energetic,
evangelical, and revolutionary half of the Reformation—
of what has been well called the "radical Reformation."[2]
Against this background, in fact, Milton's position on the
Trinity is not radical in the least. He preserves as care-
fully as any of the more "conservative" reformers a role
for Christ as "the one mediator between God and man"
(Works, 14:191), the special agent of grace and reconciliation: "Wherefore there was no grace decreed for
man who was to fall, no mode of reconciliation with God
independently of the foreknown sacrifice of Christ"
(Works, 14:105).

Milton's differences from Calvin have been at least as
interesting to scholarship as his supposed "heresies," and
the independence of his position on the freedom of the
will has been discussed in detail, commonly with a view
to showing resemblances to the doctrines of Arminianism.
I have suggested in an earlier chapter that one should
beware of supposing the Arminians hostile to the main
tendencies of the Reformation or devoted to the overthrow of Calvin. It will suffice for present purposes, however, to point out that Milton's views on the will are not
inconsistent with the formulations of the Second Helvetic
Confession, which described the faith of Calvinism in
Reformed Churches through much of Europe. Article IX,
On Free Will, declares that the sinner sins by his own will
and under no divine compulsion. The positive corollary
of this doctrine which Milton held—that the will,
prompted by grace, is capable of cooperating in regenera-

2. George H. Williams, *The Radical Reformation* (London, 1962).

tion—differs from Luther's and Augustine's position, but finds encouragement in Calvin and energetic advocacy in Melanchthon.

Milton's comments on predestination have likewise been thought to show an Arminian liberality in extending salvation to all who believe and denying the harsh Calvinist doctrine of reprobation, or predestination to damnation. But Article X of the Helvetic Confession is similarly liberal, declining to limit salvation to the few and insisting that the eventual election of all mankind is to be hoped for. It is clear both in the *De Doctrina* and *Paradise Lost* that Milton believes there to be differences between himself and Calvin worth insisting on, and he appears bent on setting a doctrinal issue straight in his repeated rather scornful references in the poem to the (Calvinist) "Decrees" of God: "As if Predestination over-rul'd / Thir will, dispos'd by absolute Decree" (III, 114–15). But this is not the only face of Calvinism, and some of its defenders take positions, in its name, that are very close to Milton's. John Edwards, writing at the end of the seventeenth century, is a Calvinist who claims that

> none who espouse predestination hold that the Decrees lay any Force or Necessity on any Man; but they all consent in this, that the Actions of Vicious Persons are Free and Voluntary, and therefore none, tho' never so Vicious, can possibly lay their Fault on Destiny and the Decrees. Man's Damnation is entirely owing to themselves as their Salvation is to God. For no Persons are damned but for their own wilful Faults, and none are saved but by the Grace of God. This is the unanimous Assertion of all Calvinists.[3]

3. John Edwards, *Theologia Reformata, or the Body and Substance of the Christian Religion* (1713), p. iv.

Arguments for Milton's Arminianism are not made
easier by his views on merit, a "doctrine" to which, he
makes clear, he would not "lend any support": for it
cannot be imagined that God "has regarded righteousness even in the least degree" in determining man's
salvation *(Works,* 15:337, 14:129). There is for Milton,
as for his Reformation forbears, no merit in man for
God to weigh. Sin, arriving in Book X at the newly
marred Creation, gloats over a future in which she will
run through all humanity and "all infect," until *(De
Doctrina,* I, iv) "all man be dead in sin" *(Works,* 14:129)
and the idea of righteousness has become a sinful self-
deception. Milton relies, then, first and last on the Reformation formula of *sola fide.* But even faith does not
make us the less sinners in the eyes of God whose way of
saving us is to forgive us. Man's sins are remitted because
of God's willingness to accept the righteousness of Christ
in place of the expiation that man cannot perform, and
Milton counters Calvin with the insistence (already met
in Luther) that we are saved *because* we are sinners—
to the slight prejudice of the elect: "So far indeed is this
satisfaction [that made by Christ] from regarding the
elect alone ... that the very contrary is the case; it regards
all sinners whatever, and it regards the elect in so far as
they were previously sinners" *(Works,* 15:327). If Miltonic
doctrine here departs from Calvinist, plainly it does not
depart from familiar Reformation ground.[4] It emphasizes
the counterpull and tension in the relationship of man

4. In fact, Milton's differences from Calvin on this point are less
than he supposes. Cf. *Institutes,* 3.xiv.5, where Calvin argues for the
necessity of sin with the support of the usual texts: "I am not come
to call the righteous but sinners" (Rom. 11: 6). "If sinners only are
admitted, why do we seek to enter by a counterfeit righteousness?"
(Matt. 9: 13).

and God which was vivid to the Reformation, and it maintains the energy of the reconciling impulse with which the God imagined by Reformation piety overcomes that tension.

On the other side, however, Milton has seemed to some readers to leave Reformation darkness for Renaissance and Arminian light in giving honor to reason. Adam is taught repeated lessons in respect for reason's government —damaged though it is and incomplete after the Fall. And Milton declares in the *De Doctrina* that "the gift of reason has been implanted in all" men, with which to discipline their wills and stiffen themselves against the impulses of disobedience *(Works,* 14:129). He goes so far in this rational enthusiasm as to say, in what appears to be a vein of high humanism, that "there are some remnants of the divine image left in man" (ibid.). But the language can be almost exactly duplicated in Calvin, who finds "seeds of divinity," "vestiges of God" in man, and suggests that those "rapid motions of the soul, its noble faculties and excellent talents, discover a Divinity not easily concealed."[5] Both cite man's rational advantages rather in reproach than in compliment. And Calvin, like Milton, compares reason in its fallen state with the right reason with which unfallen man had been blessed: "but now alienated from right reason he is almost like the cattle of the field."[6] Both consider that the renewal of faith can rectify reason again[7]—hence Milton's

---

5. *Institutes,* 1.v.4.

6. *Commentary on Genesis,* trans. Rev. John King, 2 vols. (Edinburgh, 1847), 1: 242.

7. Calvin consistently associates regeneration with knowledge: "When God illuminates us with the knowledge of himself, he is said to raise us from death, and to make us new creatures" *(Institutes,* 3.xiv.5).

urgency in pushing Reformation forward in *Areopagitica*
—and both imagine the new condition as applying not
simply to "the rational part of the soul which philos-
ophers extol, but to that which is illuminated by the
Spirit of God, so that it stands and *wills* aright" (italics
added).[8] In short, the same turning in love to meet God's
love that the Reformation never ceases to describe.

In the *De Doctrina,* as in *Paradise Lost,* reconciliation is
a main theme and God's mercy his principle characteristic. Even predestination, in Milton's understanding of
it, is "the effect of his mercy and love and grace," not at
all an arbitrary effect of his will. Its purpose is salvation
(Works, 14:99, 105) and that God might, as in Romans 9,
"make known the riches of his glory on the vessels of
his mercy" (ibid., p. 103). He is "WONDERFUL and IN-
COMPREHENSIBLE" (ibid., p. 61), beyond understanding
especially in his tenderness toward his erring creature,
who receives love though deserving wrath: "It is of the
mercies of Jehovah that we are not consumed" (ibid., p.
59). Those mercies are inseparable, Milton repeats, from
a God who has demonstrated his "infinite mercy and
grace in Christ," who is "most gracious," who extends
himself so far in love to men as to remove "the stony
from thir hearts" by "Prevenient Grace" in the first
step of a process of salvation which he continues to final
glorification entirely through his own urge to reconciliation. For God has no need of man or what man can
do *(Works,* 17:23), and "the restoration of man is purely
of grace" *(Works,* 15:339).

That the wonder of this surpassed human imagining
and staggered reason was a problem to which the sons of

8. *Commentary on Romans,* trans. Rev. John Owens (Edinburgh,
1849), p. 274. There is a valuable discussion of this aspect of Calvin's
teaching in T. F. Torrance, *Calvin's Doctrine of Man* (London,
1949), pp. 116–27.

the Reformation persistently addressed themselves. The human perception of divine purposes was in constant need of correction, and its inadequacies were, of course, understood as an evidence of fallenness. Sinful man, as a necessity of his nature, takes up positions which are, implicitly or explicitly, against God, justifying himself with arguments that faith must overthrow. Milton, as much as the other poets of this study, shows that the "mind" of the time was deeply absorbed in that dialogue and drama and impatient of neutrality. The *De Doctrina* quotes St. Paul (Rom. 9:20) for all in admonishing "Nay but, O Man, who art Thou that repliest against God?"[9]

9. *Works,* 14:147.

Index